ORDINARY MADE EXTRAORDINARY

ORDINARY MADE EXTRAORDINARY

24 THINGS TO MAKE USING EVERYDAY STUFF

Pascal Anson

SQUARE PEG

Published by Square Peg 2014

2 4 6 8 10 9 7 5 3 1

First published in Great Britain in 2014 by Square Peg
Vintage Books, Penguin Random House,
20 Vauxhall Bridge Road, London SW1V 2SA

www.vintage-books.co.uk

Addresses for companies within The Random House Group
Limited can be found at: www.randomhouse.co.uk/offices.htm

The Random House Group Limited Reg. No. 954009

A CIP catalogue record for this book
is available from the British Library

ISBN 9780224095969

The Random House Group Limited supports the Forest
Stewardship Council (FSC), the leading international forest-
certification organisation. Our books carrying the FSC label
are printed on FSC-certified paper. FSC is the only forest-
certification scheme supported by the leading environmental
organisations, including Greenpeace. Our paper procurement
policy can be found at www.randomhouse.co.uk/environment

Printed and bound in Italy by L.E.G.O. S.p.a.

FOREWORD: HAPPY AND PERHAPS HAPPIER

The idea that our environment can make us happy or unhappy has been well-explored over the centuries; in our time perhaps most notoriously in 2006 when 'pop philosopher' Alain de Botton published his book *The Architecture of Happiness*. His chapters gradually disclose the dubious or inconsistent ability of professionals – namely architects and particularly the Modernists such as Le Corbusier – to design buildings and places in such a way as to nurture happiness. It's ironic.

However much we covet and mean to create a lovely home, most of us will never commission the services of an architect (perhaps fortunately for our greater happiness). Wanting 'a beautiful and interesting environment', yet strapped for cash, Pascal Anson moves directly from the philosophy to the practicality of happiness, realising he 'could be happy and possibly happier if I could make my home look great for very little money'.

Some people are born with visual sensibility, with a seemingly intrinsic sense of form. But this is actually learned. What's intrinsic is not their sense of form – how could it be when we're born having seen nothing? – but their natural curiosity and habit of looking for examples of everything. These people earned their virtuosity by looking, and we can get better at looking. Pascal shows us how. His prologues to the detailed instructions for each project contain not so much rules as conceptual habits you have to develop in order to see the potential in ordinary things. Here are some principles sampled from Pascal's book and his YouTube channel. In me they prompt a kind of 'True or False?' reflex – a mental search for examples and counter-examples.

If you're going to be wrong, you should be really wrong. One of the most important principles of design is contrast – contrast allows you to see better – dark against light, big against small, near against far. So don't be half-wrong, because you won't be able to see what's right about your extreme wrong-ness.

Multiples have visual power. 'While the single object can be boring and mundane, the multiples can be graphically bold and exciting.' Supermarkets and vegetable stallholders know that lots and lots of the same form repeated can look really good. Pascal points out how it's even better if you introduce subtle variation in the members of the same set – which nature does naturally with vegetables of course.

Repair is improvement. 'My repaired shoes look much better and more beautiful than the shoes looked when they were perfect.' While this may not be a general truth, it is potentially true of anything that was ordinary in the first place.

Hate can be a powerful force for creative change. Take the worst and make it the best. This requires some analysis. Analyse what makes it the worst and change that. If it's the colour you hate, change the colour. If it's the shape, change the shape. If it's the hardness of the material, soften it. This is a very Pascal Anson type of logic.

Too much choice and too many options can really limit us. Total freedom is not liberating. Pick an option and pursue it *in extremis*.

Pretty much any object can look good when framed and hung on a wall. Sometimes it's the visual tension between an irregular or curvy object and a rectilinear frame that's satisfying. But not always – squares and rectangles look quite good framed as well. It's just another thing worth remembering about the way things look.

Finally a ground rule in relation to this book: **ask what can you do with what you already have, or can get at low cost.** If it's cheap or free, it's likely to be ordinary, and there'll almost certainly be some work to do to make it extraordinary.

We are awash with a retailed idea of 'originality', the 'unique' gift that will signal to others that you are an original and creative person. From joke souvenirs of the 'this lousy t-shirt' type to stock items available on notonthehighstreet.com ('for a life less ordinary'), gift-wares in particular

make it clear how flawed the notion of retailed originality is; applied personalisation and purchased sentiment can never be the real thing they purport to be. Pascal points out (yet without a tinge of scorn – this is a book entirely without ill-feeling) how this disingenuousness extends from gifts themselves to E-cards and the gift-wrapping and greeting-message services provided by online retailers.

So how do we get thought, sentiment, into an object? Pascal has some really good answers to this. Not by writing your name on it. Not by making it look like a favourite plant or animal. Not by inscribing it with a proverb or a joke. Look really hard at what it is. It's metal. How can I make it more metal-y? Or what if I make it the opposite? What's the opposite of metal? Look really hard at what you have. A jumble. How can I unify it and make it look like it's a set? What single thing could I do to all the parts that signals their belonging together? The result is a record of your thinking. What Pascal is concerned with nurturing, in his own words, is a combination of low skill and high design that is idiosyncratic and resourceful. The great American architect Louis Khan famously used to tell his students, 'Ask the brick what the brick wants to be'. There is something of this search for material essence in *Ordinary Made Extraordinary*. **A quest to exploit the Sellotape-ness of Sellotape (transparency and potential for layering into rigidity), the** mirror-ness of a certain kind of widely available mirror (commonality and variety within pattern), the present-ness of a present (tied by a bow – which the father of all graphic designers, Paul Rand, also intuited when he designed the original logo for UPS). Bruno Munari, one of the greatest-ever design teachers and writers, wrote of the eternal virtue of a 'cuplike-cup' and a 'tablelike-table' and a 'chairlike-chair'. Design, he meant, should not be the hapless pursuit of figurative translation so that our things look like other things or tell other people's retailed jokes, but a pursuit of their greater authenticity so that they look more like themselves. If you make a car out of wood (or make it look like it's made of wood), you do draw attention to its car-ness.

Two big ideas are the foundation of this book: one, to make something extraordinary you make it your own; two, you get from like to love by changing the way something looks. Love makes everyone happier: true or false?

Emily Campbell

ORDINARY MADE EXTRAORDINARY

INTRODUCTION

When I was little I loved making things. My mum tells me that the first really impressive thing I made was a blue Play-Doh kangaroo. I didn't really like any of the things they showed you how to make on Blue Peter, though. And I always followed the instructions on Lego exactly and so never built anything as an imaginative alternative. But I do remember always having a strong vision in my mind's eye of how spaces should look or how things could be made and how they would work.

As young children we are encouraged at school to make models, papier mâché, badges, costumes, kites, mobiles and animals, also pottery perhaps, and at the very least to get messy with paint. Then, somehow all this creativity just fizzles out. Maybe there is no need, or we change, or we simply become lazy. But, even if you don't have a creative job, I believe that creativity still lives within all of us somewhere. It is primitive human instinct to make objects that will make our lives better. Shopping and consuming has, to some extent, replaced that instinct by making access to 'things' really simple; but, in the same way that a cake, or a loaf of bread you have baked yourself just tastes better, making things makes you feel great.

When I left college in 2000 I knew I didn't want to work full time at a design practice because I didn't want to be in the position where my designs had to be commercial and make money. The most important factor in making this choice was that there should be no compromise on my own creativity. But I also realised that, without a job, I had no income and so I tried to streamline my finances to a point where I didn't need much money to live. I worked part-time at other jobs and this paid the bills. The rest of the time I experimented with different ways of designing and making things.

In 2005 I won a scholarship from The Esmée Fairbarin Foundation and the Design Museum in London. My work was shown all over the world with the British Council. I should also mention at this time that my dishwasher caught fire and my flat was completely destroyed. After it was refurbished I found myself living in a brand-new, refitted show home. Urgh. I was too scared to make a mess or a mark on any of the pristine new decor to design or make anything in it, so I had to move out.

I moved into a live-work unit outside London which needed a lot of work doing to it and I had virtually no money. There was no bathroom for several weeks and nothing was how I wanted it. Over the next few years I moved walls and made a bathroom, built staircases and installed a kitchen. The reason why the idea of the show home was so bothersome was that a perfect-looking home was never my ambition or aim.

I grew up in South London, my parents are both artists and the house always had interesting objects in it: statues from abandoned hospital grounds, reclaimed flooring, tables from schools and signs from shop-fronts. I wanted to live in a stimulating and interesting home but a lack of money forced me to find creative alternatives to the lifestyle sold to us in TV advertising, style magazines and (usually dull) makeover programmes.

I figured I could be happy, possibly even happier, if I could make my home look great for very little money. Yes, I would like a nicer car, but instead of whinging on about it or getting a loan to buy one, I transformed my existing car. Sometimes really hating what you have can be a powerful force for creative change.

I have always loved making films ever since I got a camcorder as a teenager. Narrative and storytelling in design is always something that I have wanted to experiment with. I'm now a tutor in design at Kingston University and at the Royal College of Art and I always encourage my students to make films about their work to show the context of the idea behind their project or design, or simply to show how it works. I began to make films so I could explain why I had done what I had with my house, to explain the rationale. I had no agenda, I just began trying to talk about design in a fun and creative way.

People liked my videos (and some people hated them) and that encouraged me to make some more and think of new projects to make films about. I also started a blog which I see as my online sketchbook to share and write about the things I like looking at and playing with. At this point I still wasn't making any money from my design work, but it was work I wanted to continue to do. I started setting some rules for myself: all the projects should be low skill-level, but high design. My aim was that anyone following my designs should not need access to technical machinery and that most might be achieved at home at your kitchen table.

Then, I was approached to write a book. As a child I never liked reading (I always wanted to be making or doing something, not sitting quietly) and as an adult I didn't have much confidence in my ability to write well, but nevertheless, here is the book! As you can see, it has a lot of pictures. I worked with a fantastic photographer, Mark Vessey and took over 10,000 photographs of the processes of making the things in this book. We wanted the photographs to make the 'big picture' as obvious as possible and the small details clear and easy to follow.

Some of the projects in the book are presented with step-by-step instructions for you to follow exactly, others have more leeway and you can improvise a little, and several projects are intended as springboards for you to create your own versions from. This is how I see the basic, intermediate and advanced levels in the book. Designers and artists want people to experience their work, through buying and owning their product, or looking at it in a museum. My aim with this book is to design a range of products that cover many areas of everyday life, things that normally we would just buy, and present them to you as things that you will enjoy making, will want to keep and will love using.

MATE

RIALS

EXTRAORDINARY PROJECTS FROM ORDINARY MATERIALS

Waterproof Shoes
The Sellotape Chandelier
Vacuum Chair
Cling Film Tree House

Extraordinary materials are all around us. In the garden shed, in the kitchen cupboard and in the local hardware store.

Take cling film or plastic wrap, for example. There is much more to this humble 'ordinary' everyday material than first meets the eye. Like many basic household materials, plastic wrap, or Saran Wrap to the Americans, was created by accident in a laboratory in the US almost eighty years ago. It was first used by the military as a waterproof coating for aircraft during the Second World War (it was then green and had a nasty smell) and by the automotive industry before being used in the food industry in packaging, the use we are most familiar with today. Yes, plastic wrap is used to wrap sandwiches in your packed lunch. But one roll of ordinary supermarket cling film can also be used to make a hammock strong enough to support the weight of an adult. Extraordinary!

The most common everyday materials are wood, plastic, stone and metal. These in turn can be treated or processed to make other ordinary materials. Wood becomes wood chips which are transformed into MDF (Medium Density Fibre) boards, plastic into PVC sheets, and metal into aluminium foil, for example.

Many extraordinary materials are already all around us in the guise of something so ordinary we don't give it a second glance. They are not in themselves dull but often it's the way in which we use them that has become traditional or just boring.

Most everyday or industrial materials are fit for very specific purposes but some can be more adaptable. Understanding which material suits which purpose is often common sense. Think of factors like durability, texture, warmth and perhaps the way a certain material looks. In short, how the material behaves, how it feels and what it looks like. Knowledge about materials comes from testing and experimenting, often to understand at what point a material breaks and becomes useless. Be ambitious with your experiments (even if they turn into ambitious failures). A good rule is always to ignore what it says on the tin.

In this section I'm going to take some very ordinary materials and challenge the way they are normally used. Here are a few pointers to help you see materials and their possible functions in a more extraordinary way.

1. Look again at the materials you have to hand or that are cheaply and easily available. Think of new ways you could use a particular material, transforming the ordinary into the extraordinary.

2. Experiment with materials – though trial and error you discover both a material's limits and potential new uses.

3. Turn your ideas upside down. Think of a use for a material that hasn't been attempted before. In other words, think like a designer.

These first four projects use readily available materials in ways that perhaps you haven't thought about before. In each project, the intended use for the material tries to move as far away as possible from its everyday use. As with all the projects in this book, the skill level required is relatively low, but the design and idea content is high.

WATERPROOF SHOES

'This project is about
practicality and
fashion... it rains
a lot in the UK'

ORDINARY MADE EXTRAORDINARY

It rains a lot in the UK and I do not own a pair of wellington boots – I wear trainers most of the time and this means that I often end up with wet feet. The idea for these waterproof shoes came to me soon after getting some dipping rubber called Plasti Dip. It comes in bright primary colours (including glow-in-the-dark), air dries and gives a great finish and it got me thinking of all the different things I could possibly dip.

Around the same time, the Swedish plimsole manufacturer Tretorn was asking designers to customise their basic plimsoles.

I wanted to do something functional rather than decorative and I noticed that the toe of the plimsole wasn't rubber-capped – which would mean wet toes on rainy days. So I chose to dip the shoes in yellow dipping rubber to waterproof them but also to add an aesthetic dimension to this classic white sports shoe.

INGREDIENTS

- plastic bags
- shoes
- hooks
- paper
- Plasti Dip®

1. Make sure the room is well ventilated – the Plasti Dip® is quite pungent! Push several plastic bags into the toes of your plimsoles, and hang them from a rail over a table, as shown.

2. & 3. Place some paper under the shoes to catch drips and protect the table surface. Pour some Plasti Dip® into a suitable container. Hold the shoe steady with one hand, and with the other, raise the filled container to the shoe. Carefully and slowly dip the toe of the shoe into the rubber paint.

4. Again, slowly and steadily lower the container from the dipped shoe-tip.

5. Repeat with the other shoe.

6. Leave the shoes to drip-dry thoroughly.

THE
SELLOTAPE
CHANDELIER

'I'm going to show
you how to make this
chandelier with ten
rolls of Sellotape'

ORDINARY MADE EXTRAORDINARY

This project is about using a simple everyday material, Sellotape, in an unusual way to exploit two of its unique properties.

First, because it is sticky on one side, you can mould it round a form really quickly and effectively. Second, it is transparent and refracts light in an interesting way. Finding a material that is right for an application is a skill that takes knowledge and experience, but finding a material that is uniquely appropriate to a certain function is very difficult. I think that using Sellotape in this way is getting there.

I needed a starting point with this project, so I used an existing chandelier on which to base my design. I assembled several unrelated components, a traffic cone, some bowls and a tray and then gaffer taped them together to form approximately the right shape.

In a similar way to the Pallet Replica Armchair on p.112, I am not suggesting that you necessarily make an exact copy of this chandelier, more that you follow the rationale and process and play with the idea shown here.

Before I started on the actual chandelier, I did a couple of tests with the Sellotape on a salad bowl so I could see how the material behaved. In most projects, testing is critical to success. This is quite an ambitious project; you are using Sellotape in a way that you probably haven't before. My tips for success are to be methodical, take your time and make sure you have enough rolls of tape to complete your project.

INGREDIENTS

- 10 rolls Sellotape
- salad bowl
- craft knife
- traffic cone
- scissors
- tray
- gaffer tape
- plastic cup
- dessert bowl
- tea light holder
- ping-pong ball
- low energy light bulb

Visualise how you might assemble various ordinary
objects to create the form for your chandelier.

1. You will need a large bowl (I used a salad bowl), a roll of Sellotape and a sharp knife.

2. Wrap the tape sticky-side up to cover the whole surface and the top of the bowl.

3. Check that the tape has covered the surface entirely, then flip the tape over and start wrapping the tape sticky-side down.

4. Continue to wrap until there are no sticky bits of tape on the entire surface. Using a sharp knife, cut round the inside edge of the bowl.

5. Remove the circle of tape from the top of the bowl.

6. Gently, but firmly, ease out the bowl and you will have a replica bowl made from Sellotape.

Now that you've perfected the bowl, try moving on to this chandelier...

1. Assemble all the objects you will use as a mould for the different elements of your chandelier.

2. Remove the reflective plastic from the traffic cone.

3. Remove the base from the traffic cone, using a craft knife or strong scissors.

4. Cut some tabs at the base of the cone.

5. Position the cone in the centre of the tray and press down firmly so the tabs splay out.

6. Join the traffic cone to the tray, using strong gaffer tape.

7. Cut the top off the cone.

8. & 9. Attach the small dessert bowl to the top of the cone and fit the plastic cup inside the bowl. Tape all the pieces together securely. Don't worry about it being TOO neat.
10. Position the tray on top of the large salad bowl.

11. Tape securely together.
12. Attach the tea light holder and the ping-pong ball to the base of the salad bowl. The mould for your chandelier is now ready.

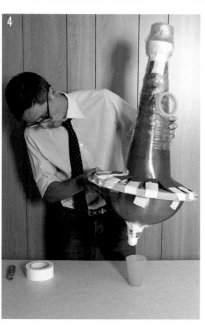

1. Starting near the middle of the traffic cone, wrap the firmly Sellotape around it, STICKY-SIDE OUT.

2. Continue to wrap the tape over itself sticky-side out. Again don't worry about neatness.

3. Once the tape is secure, start to wrap up and down the top part of the mould.

4. To prevent the mould rolling about as you wrap, place the base in a cup.

5. Start to wrap the bottom of your mould, again with the Sellotape sticky-side out. This is the trickiest bit and it can help to have an extra pair of hands to hold the mould steady for you as you wrap.

6. Work methodically, rotating the mould to work steadily around the base.

7. Cover the whole surface of the mould at least twice, with the Sellotape sticky-side out.

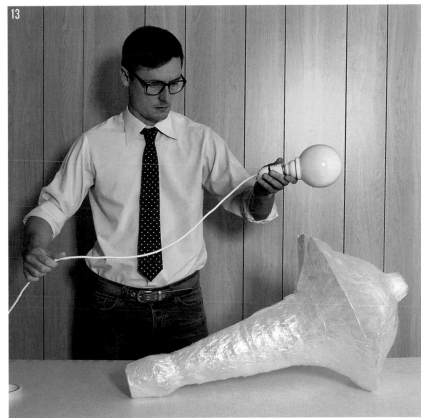

8. Then flip the tape over and start to wrap methodically, smooth-side out, so that all the sticky surface is slowly but surely covered.

9. This bit is much faster and easier. Cover the entire surface with at least two more layers of tape, smooth-side out.

10. Check that there are no missed sticky bits. If there are, cover with more tape.

11. With a sharp knife, cut down in a straight line down one whole side of the form.

12. Carefully ease the tape structure away from the mould.

13. Place a low energy light bulb inside the bottom dome of the Sellotape chandelier. To finish, use more tape to wrap all around to close the chandelier at the cut.

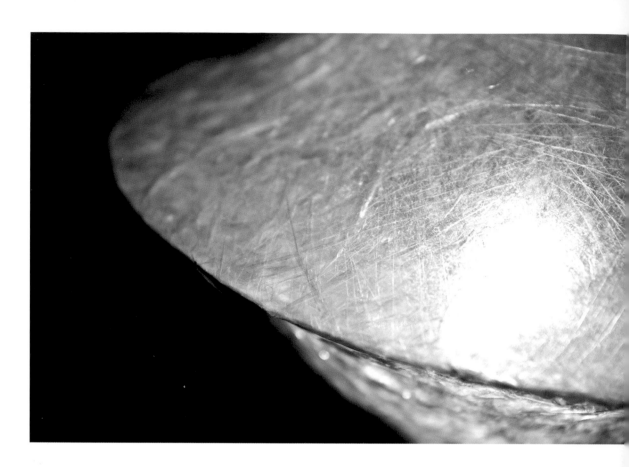

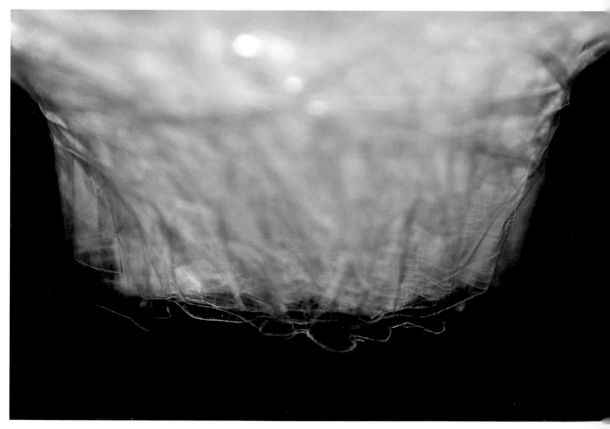

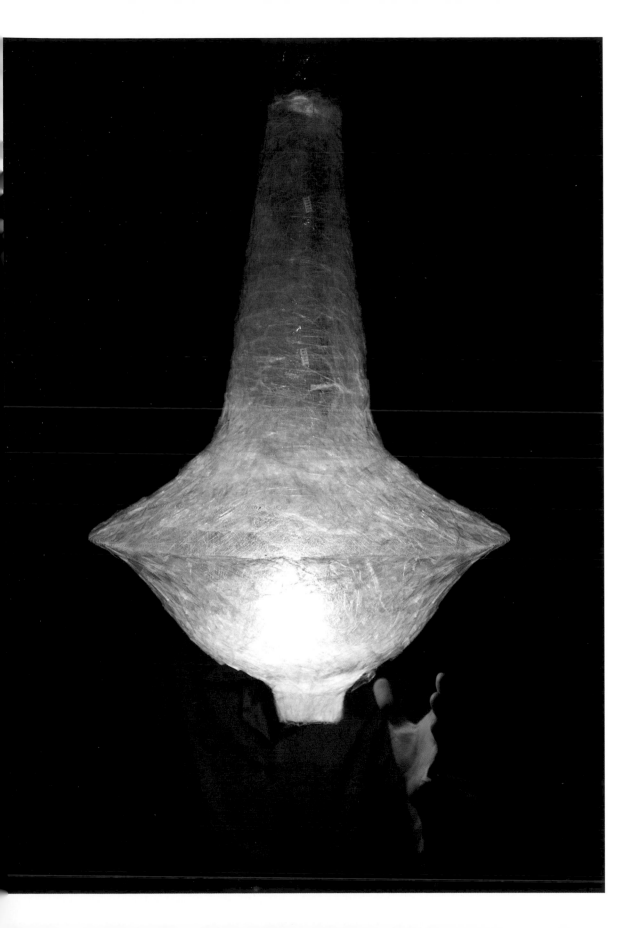

VACUUM CHAIR

'I hate those linen-covered dining chairs like the ones you get at weddings'

INGREDIENTS

- plastic sheeting (e.g. Mylar®)
- double-sided tape
- epoxy glue
- hair comb
- vacuum cleaner

Inspiration for design can come from many different sources. I really dislike those dining chairs that you often see in marquees at weddings – the ones that get covered in a fabric drape. So here is what I am suggesting as an alternative. This project transforms the old and dated wooden chair into something which looks very space age.

There have been a few projects using vacuums but I wanted to take it one step further and use glue to make the result more permanent. I am always amazed at the amount of pressure a regular domestic vacuum cleaner can generate.

I don't think that this project is at all dangerous but a few tests did implode because of the pressure, so if you hear a really loud bang...don't worry, it's just the vacuum sucking a hole out of the plastic foil! I used Mylar®, which is available from gardening supply shops and comes on a roll. For the glue, I used an epoxy two-part adhesive from my local model shop. Drawing the air out of the foil bag also distributes the glue nicely around the chair and the foil ends up sticking to itself and also to the chair to give the dramatic effect. The end result will be different each time and you can also try it with other objects. You don't need a special vacuum cleaner.

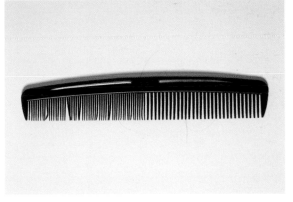

1. Work on a large table. Fold a large piece of Mylar® (or similar) plastic sheeting in half, shiny side down as shown, and crease it at the fold. I used a 300cm x 125cm sheet.
2. Unfold the sheet.
3. Attach strong double-sided tape along the long sides, but do not remove the backing.
4. Fold it back in half.

5. Cut through both thicknesses of the plastic at the open end, leaving a tab as shown. Unfold the sheet again. Attach double-sided tape to the inside short edge and to the sides of the tab, leaving only the end of the tab untaped.
6. Mix about 500ml liquid epoxy glue in a container.

7. Pour the glue over one half of the plastic sheeting.

8. & 9. Use a comb to spread the glue evenly over the whole surface of only this half.

10. Fold over the uncoated half of the sheet and smooth down.

11. Remove the backing from the double-sided tape on the long sides and seal securely.

12. Insert your ordinary chair.

13. Lift the bag up slightly to help the chair slide in easily.

14. Remove the backing from the double-sided tape at the open end.

15. Seal all the edges together carefully.

16. Insert the nozzle of your vacuum cleaner into the tab opening and switch it on!

CLING FILM TREE HOUSE

'Be ambitious and careful with your structure, and clear up afterwards!'

INGREDIENTS

- stepladder
- cling film

Most of us have a roll of cling film in our kitchen drawer. But have you ever thought that you could make a simple structure such as a hammock or a tree house from it? I wanted to be really ambitious and create a large tree house in the forest. Using cling film. The surprising strength of the structure relies on multiple layers of film, pulled tightly, and using trees as solid anchors at the four corners. I found that a systematic approach worked best in terms of the wrapping and very quickly a completely enclosed and elevated structure was starting to take shape. Here's how we did it.

I needed a bit of help with this, but you really don't have to be an architect to get it right. I wanted to use four trees as my starting point, but you might want to use more or just three to form the basic structure. If you're still not convinced that cling film is really strong enough to make a tree house, try a much smaller project like a hammock to start with. Take care and test for strength before you climb in.

1. Start to wrap the cling film around four trees at about waist level. Depending on the thickness of the cling film, continue to wrap, making about eight to ten circuits of the trees.

2. Keep the cling film tension steady and taut, with no slack, especially as you round each corner.

3. Standing on a step ladder, start to wrap a second level of cling film as in Step 1., about 1m above the first. Again, keep the cling film taut and add about eight or ten layers.

4. Start to wrap the cling film across two opposite sides on the bottom level, pulling it taut to create the 'floor' of your tree house.

5. Add four to five layers of cling film – the sides will pull in significantly, as shown.

6. Repeat across the other sides of the square. You will have a total thickness of ten layers of film.

7. Again, with the help of the step ladder, wrap over the higher level and the sides to create a roof and tree house sides, leaving an opening clear.

8. Cling film can also be used to join smaller branches together to make a ladder.

9. Test the strength and safety of your creation before inviting small people inside.

EXTRAORDINARY PROJECTS FROM ORDINARY SHOPPING

Soft Furnishings
Mirror Wall
The Mismatched Fitted Kitchen
Cool Dad-Jeans

I love shopping but dislike buying things. I try to be extremely careful with money as it doesn't come easily. There are so many nice things to buy, with new and tempting products appearing at an ever increasing pace.

When I first made my '4 Minute Skinny Jeans' video and posted it on YouTube, it struck me that we now live in a time where a pair of standard supermarket jeans costs the same as a pint of beer, a couple of chicken breasts, or fifteen-minute train journey. I find this at once strange, horrible, disturbing and amazing, yet somehow accept it as a completely normal state of affairs. Retailers have become so finely tuned to our desires as consumers that I think it's now time for us to turn the tables and take advantage of how things are sold rather than retailers making a killing out of our acquisitive nature.

Perhaps the consumerist tide is slowly beginning to turn. More and more of us are making stuff ourselves. Just look at the popularity of online sites such as Etsy and Folksy, and the street food and craft market revolution. Yes, 21st-century shopping has given us seemingly limitless options for buying but sometimes still we need to make things ourselves and take pride in making them well, whether it be a pot of jam, a cake or a shirt. Making things is part of our nature too.

Shopping can make us lazy and spend more money than we really need to. The projects in this chapter look at shopping for things a little differently with ideas for buying cheaply and transforming, modifying and tweaking your purchase to make it into something just a little more unique.

SOFT FURNISHINGS

'£100 for a cashmere cushion cover? You have to be kidding'

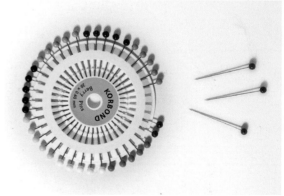

ORDINARY MADE EXTRAORDINARY

It's all very well being able to buy cashmere sweaters at the supermarket now, but often the cashmere is quite thin (one ply), does not survive long after being washed or gets eaten by moths. I've noticed that cashmere cushion covers cost a lot of money – sometimes as much as £100. £100 for a cushion cover? That's wrong, right?

When your supermarket sweater is past its best and the elbows have gone, here's what to do with the garment. Chop the arms off, sew up the neckline and sew a zip at the waist. You'll have a very cosy cushion in no time.

INGREDIENTS

- jumper
- pins
- cushion pad
- card
- chalk
- sewing machine
- thread
- scissors
- zip

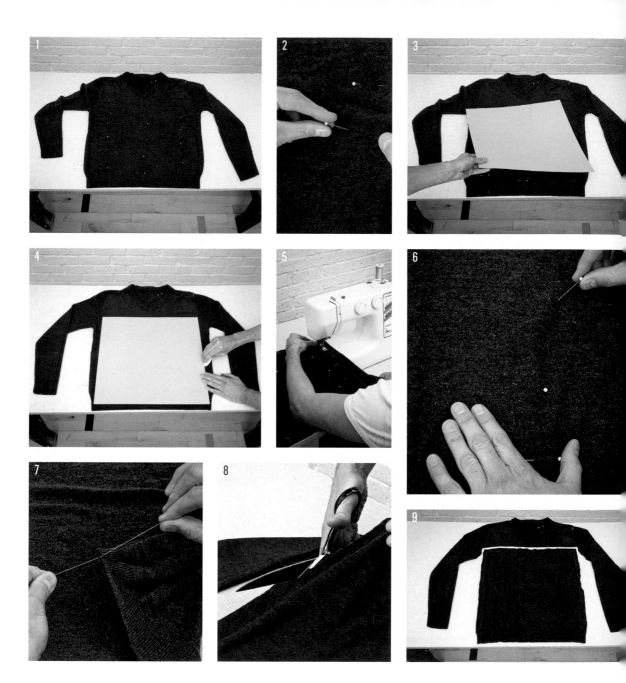

1. Turn your sweater inside out and place it on a flat surface. Pin the front to the back.
2. Space the pins every 5cm to secure the two sides firmly and prevent the fabric slipping.
3. Measure your cushion pad and cut a piece of thick paper to these dimensions. Place the card on the pinned sweater.

4. Use tailor's chalk to mark around the edges of the card.
5. Sew along the chalk line on three of the sides, leaving the bottom of the sweater open.
6. Remove the pins.
7. Tie off the ends to secure the stitching.
8. Use sharp dressmaking scissors or pinking shears to cut off excess fabric round the sides, about 1cm from the seams.

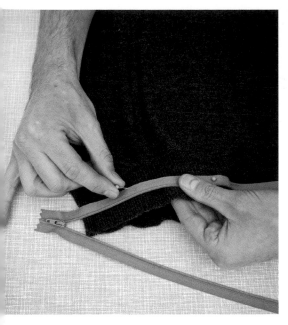

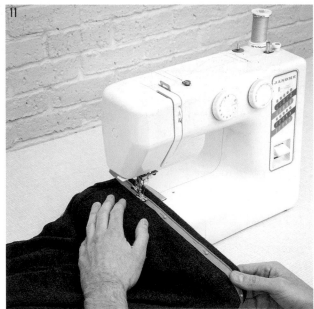

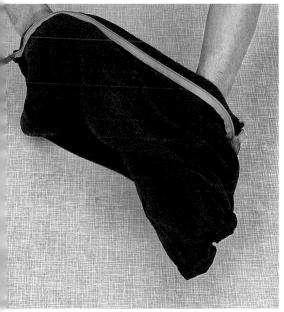

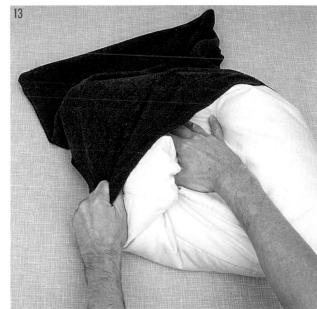

9. You should have a square like this. Do not wear the excess material as a garment!

10. Pin a zip of suitable length 2cm from the open hem of the sweater on both sides.

11. Tack on the zip by hand, remove the pins then carefully sew on the zip by machine.

12. Turn the sweater-cushion cover right-side out.

13. Stuff in your cushion pad and zip to close.

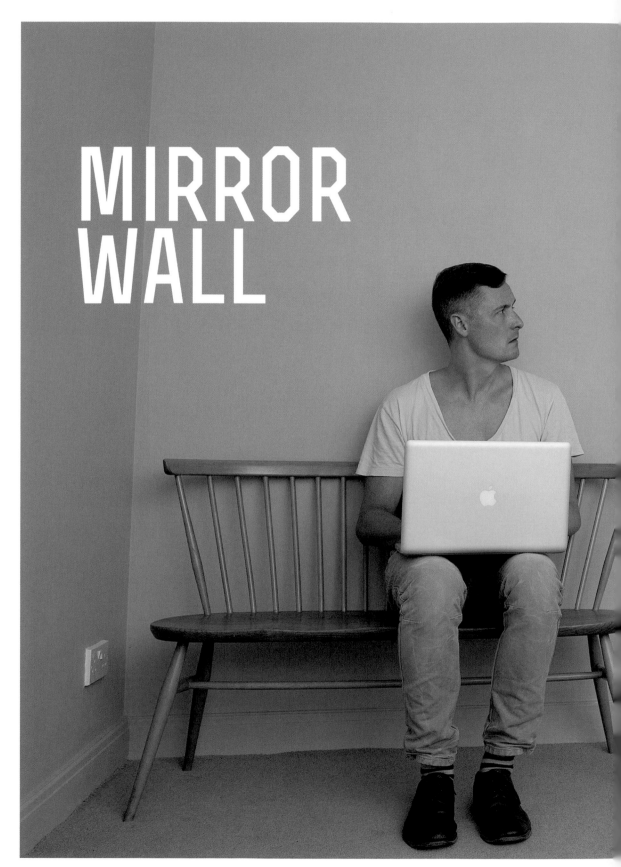

MIRROR
WALL

Artists have used multiples to create visual impact for a long time: Andy Warhol's Campbell's Soup Cans and Brillo packaging pieces spring to mind. Multiples and repetition of one thing or a similar thing mean that a work on a large scale can quickly achieved. This project uses this principle, but is also about collecting within a certain rule set.

Every collection starts with one or possibly two similar things. I live and work in an art deco-style studio (art-deco style was revived in the 1950s) and I bought a 1950s' mirror for my hallway. I then found a nicer one a few weeks later, so I hung it instead in the hall. I then had to find somewhere else to hang the first one. In the small hallway, the mirror had looked good. On its own on a large wall, it looked a bit lost. So I started to keep an eye out for other 1950s' art-deco mirrors and gradually, over the next few years, after looking in charity and junk shops and on eBay, I managed to fill a whole wall.

What I really love is the variation in each mirror in terms of shape and outline. Each one has the characteristic bevelled edge, and they are all similar in size, but I have never seen two of these mirrors that are exactly the same. This makes me wonder about the manufacturing of objects in the 1950s compared to today, when everyone seems to have the same bookcases, cutlery and lamps from Ikea.

When I hung the mirrors up I tried to make sure that the distance from one to another was as even as I could make it. Each mirror cost under £10, so while twenty mirrors in one go would seem expensive, spread over a couple of years it was easily affordable. And it's great fun to keep your eye out for that perfect addition to your evolving collection project.

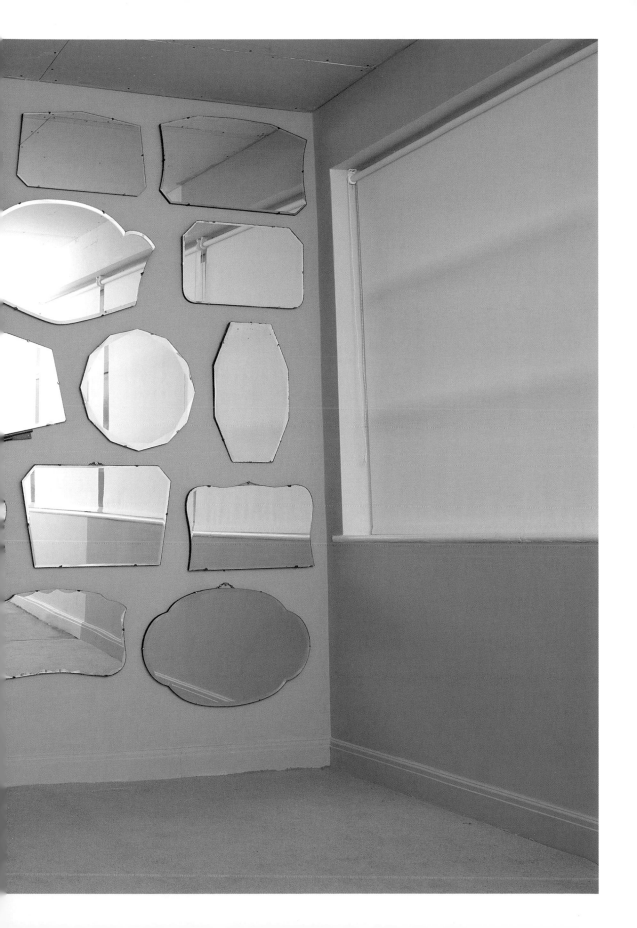

THE MISMATCHED FITTED KITCHEN

'Kitchen manufacturers make money on the doors, not the cabinets'

I have designed and fitted quite a few Ikea kitchens for friends and family. My mum and I went to the Toulouse Ikea to buy a few units to make the most of the space she has in her tiny kitchen in France. And when my friend Yuko moved from Tokyo to Milan and her kitchen had pipes coming out from the wall, we hired a van and off we went to Milan's Ikea to buy her some cupboard units. (It was the most stressful weekend of my life.) My rented flat in London burned down because of an electrical fault in the dishwasher just a few weeks after I'd installed an Ikea kitchen there, so a few weeks later the same configuration was installed again.

So, I think it's fair to say that I know Ikea kitchens fairly well. When I needed a kitchen for my own home, I really had a very limited budget. I knew that the kitchen manufacturers must make their money on the doors to the cabinets, not the cabinets themselves (which are comparatively cheap) so I thought about just buying the cabinets, and then, when I had enough money, buying doors to put on them.

On my trip to Ikea to buy the cabinets, I spotted a lot of single unpackaged door fronts in the bargain corner – presumably they were from show kitchens or returns. They were very cheap,

ranging from £1 to £6. None of them matched, so I decided to find fourteen different door fronts.

To begin with I used them just as they were. Later I decided to paint them all the same colour, then spray painted each of the door handles in a different colour.

INGREDIENTS

- doors
- knobs
- paint
- paintbrush
- spray paints

1. Go to the clearance section of your nearest Scandinavian Furniture Store and, if possible, select a different door to fit each of your kitchen units.

2. Paint all the doors the same colour. I recommend a nice boring, neutral grey.

3. Remove the old doors from the existing units, or if starting from scratch, install the units in your kitchen.

4. Fit a new door to each cabinet unit.

5. Make sure that you have a really good mismatch, with no two identical doors adjoining.

6. Paint some small door knobs in different
colours using spray paints, as shown.
7. Check that the doors are well aligned.
8. Attach the painted door knobs.

COOL DAD-JEANS

'What does £5 buy?'

I have a question... How come more of us don't think that it is completely weird that you can buy a pair of jeans in the supermarket for about the same price as a pack of chicken thighs? It seems that no one really notices. It seems perfectly normal. I asked some acquaintances who work in fashion why it is that we can buy such cheap jeans now and the answers were a little different to what I expected.

It is not always that the jeans are made in sweatshop conditions, or that they are poor quality; sometimes the material was wrong in the first instance, or it could be that the stock is surplus to an order, a huge bankrupt stock of cut-price jeans. And that is why there are £5 jeans in our local supermarkets. Jeans can also cost you £50 or £100 or £500 with perhaps only small discernable differences.

The jeans I bought at the supermarket were well made and the denim was good quality. The problem was the fit: they looked like jeans my dad would wear. Dad jeans. I am by no means a denim snob, so I tried some different clothes on to feel better about wearing them. Still bad. Then I just sewed another seam in the inside of the leg. Simple.

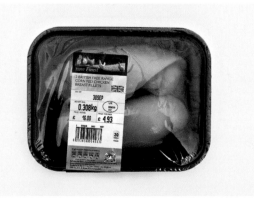

It works on both men's and women's jeans...and you don't have to cut the seam out, which means that the change is temporary and you can alter them back when fashion changes. Or you grow into your dad. It's incredibly easy and only takes five minutes.

INGREDIENTS

- supermarket jeans
- nice jeans
- felt-tip pen or tailor's chalk
- pins
- sewing machine

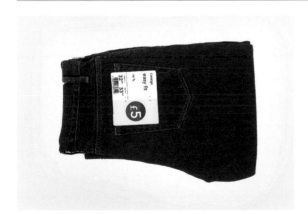

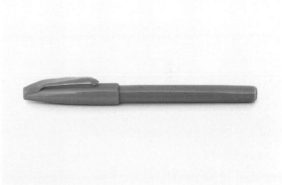

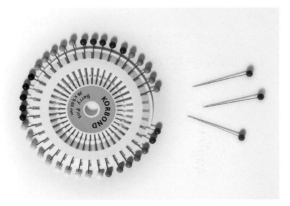

1. Turn your uncool jeans inside out.
2. Place them flat on the floor.
3. Position your best-fitting, skinnier jeans over the top.
4. Align the two pairs of jeans to ensure that the outer-leg seams match exactly.

5. Trace a line along the skinny jeans' inside-leg seam with a felt tip or tailor's chalk – you will sew along this line to create a new seam on the uncool jeans.
6. Check that the marked lines match up to meet at the crotch.
7. Remove the skinny jeans and pin all the way round about 1cm from the new marked seam-line.

8. Start from the bottom of the leg and sew all along the traced seam-line opening.

9. Use the reverse button to sew over a few times at the bottom leg opening to reinforce and secure the stitching.

10. This also applies when you get to the crotch area.

11. Remove the pins.

12. Tie off the ends to secure and snip off any extra thread for a tidy finish. There is no need to trim the excess fabric on the inside, as this allows you to undo the stitching should uncool jeans come back into fashion and you need to change the shape of the jeans again.

EXTRAORDINARY PROJECTS FROM ORDINARY UNWANTED

The New Set
Butterfly Shoes
The Ugly Table
Pallet Replica Armchair

I love car boot sales and looking in charity, thrift and junk shops; I probably get this from my dad. When I was very young I didn't like second-hand stuff much, but when I was a student it was the only way to afford clothes, objects and furniture which were not only cheap but also a bit different or even a one-off.

If you keep your eyes open you'll see discarded treasures all over the place, not just in junk shops: on the roadside and in skips, or at the recycling depot, though you might not strike gold on the first visit (you might have to go ten times before you do). I get a huge thrill from finding something that has been discarded and imagining what the possibilities for its reinvention might be. I love the sense that I've found a gem, that someone had overlooked its merits and was stupid enough to throw it away. Their oversight is my gain. Seeing the potential in unwanted items takes imagination and often a bit of problem-solving – you have to change your way of thinking to see the opportunity in stuff that others might consider junk.

This chapter is about looking at unwanted objects differently, either by taking them apart and reconfiguring them or by changing their appearance or use. Ask yourself: what if I painted this? Turned it upside down? Or joined it with another item to make it useful in a new way?

Yes, this is up-cycling of a kind, but I want you to be a bit more creative than simply sticking some flowers in an old milk bottle. That's far too twee.

THE
NEW
SET

'Re-unifying orphaned pieces of cutlery to form a new family'

This is the original project that got me started on this phase of work. When I was at the Royal College of Art we each had our own toolbox. Of course, people borrow tools and invariably bits and pieces go missing. I decided to dip the handles of all my tools in red fluorescent paint to mark them as belonging to my set, and to increase the chance of borrowed items making their way back to my toolbox. It worked, up to a point. But in addition, the disparate contents of my toolbox – from my granddad's old tools to stuff I got from the pound shop – suddenly looked like a complete set. By dipping all the handles red, I had unified them into a new set. It hadn't

been a conscious decision or a new project; it was just a solution to the problem of my tools going missing.

My tutors at the time were Jasper Morrison and Michael Marriott and they pointed out that this was an interesting direction. So I moved on to unifying other sets of disparate things: odd bits of crockery, chairs and cutlery. These sets were later shown at the Design Museum in London in 2005 and then selected to travel internationally in an exhibition called Great Brits.

This project is something that anyone can do, and you can apply the idea to any kinds of objects. For me the unification/reunification projects are about regrouping lost or orphaned pieces, rather than buying new. What you end up with is the detail and rich difference of many different designs, but with the added cohesion and unity of a set.

INGREDIENTS

- cutlery
- gaffer tape
- Plasti Dip®

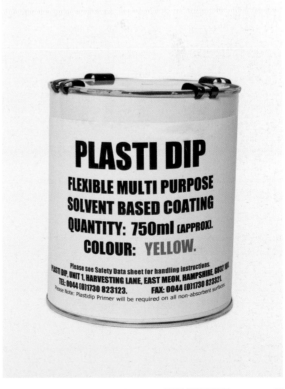

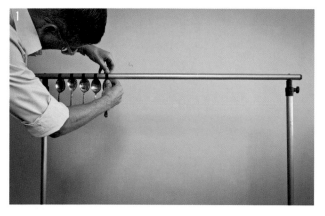

1. & 2. Hang up your first piece of mismatched cutlery (I used gaffer tape), handle down, along a rail or a rack, as shown. Cover the floor below with newspaper to catch the drips. Raise the pot of Plasti Dip® and dip the handle to the desired point.

3. Slowly lower the pot, catching the excess dipping paint.

4. Repeat, hanging and dipping each piece of cutlery at a time.

5. One coat works best, so the original detail on each handle is still visible.

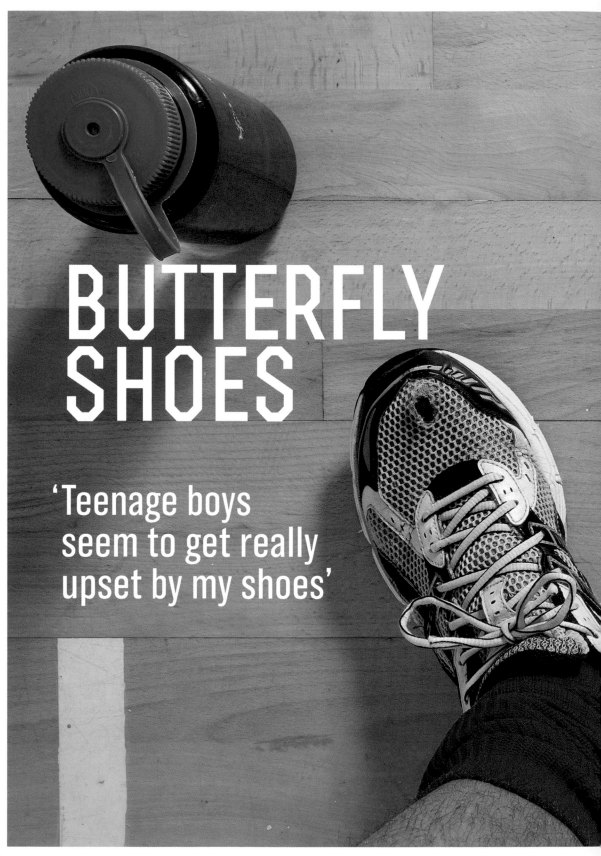

BUTTERFLY SHOES

'Teenage boys seem to get really upset by my shoes'

I like sport. I like keeping fit and it is very important to buy good running shoes to look after your feet and knees. When I walk or run, I must poke my big toe upwards as my foot rolls forward because I have noticed that I start to break through the toes of shoes after a certain amount of time. These particular shoes have a light mesh and very quickly there was a hole with my big toe poking through. Maybe I need to cut my toenails more often, but I know it isn't just me who ends up with trainers in this state!

This is what I ended up doing to repair my running shoes. I wanted to use iron-on patches to fix them. I searched online and chose butterflies over strawberries or ponies. I had been inspired by a dragonfly landing on my foot whilst I was lying in the park, and wondered what the insect must have been thinking that it had landed on. I'm fascinated by the way that animals and insects perceive the same world we inhabit in a totally different way. I had to buy quite a lot of iron-on butterflies. I repaired the hole and then kept adding and adding more of the patches by sewing them to the shoes. Initially this was to stop the repair looking like a patch-up, and then I got carried away and imagined a whole swarm of butterflies on my shoes.

INGREDIENTS

- trainers
- socks
- iron
- patches
- cloth
- needle
- thread

The end result is that the running shoes are transformed both in look and purpose – something sporty and practical into shoes which are no longer suitable for running. I like the contrast of the technical trainers with the butterfly aesthetic. Teenage boys particularly hate them, I think, because I've subverted the culture they think they own. Small girls love them but are confused by why a grown man would wear such things. I am very happy with both these reactions.

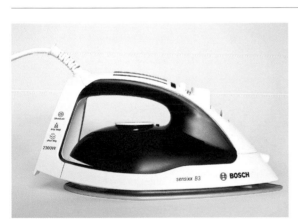

1. Stuff a pair of socks into the toes of your worn-out running shoes and turn an iron on to high.

2. Position one of the iron-on patches over the hole in the shoe.

3. Place a small piece of clean cotton fabric over the patch to prevent the iron from scorching it.

4. Press down firmly on the patch with the hot iron.

5. Repeat the steps above to cover any further holes and then continue to iron on more patches as desired.

6. You can also sew on further patches by hand to create a more textured effect.

7. Don't worry about making the left and right shoe match.

THE
UGLY
TABLE

'If something
looks awkward,
cut it in half.
It might then look
half as awkward'

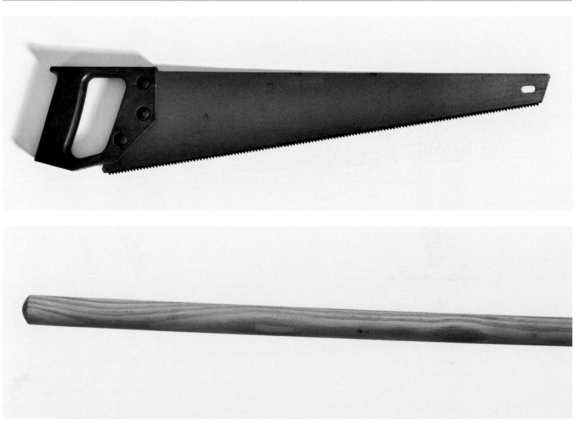

I am always on the look-out for interesting things to make other things from. I found this table discarded on the pavement. My first reaction was that it was horrible, compounded by the fact that it was a bit dirty and someone else had thrown it out. Then I thought of it as a challenge to see what I might be able to turn it into. Finally I decided that simply cutting it in half would reduce its fussy form which seemed to occupy too much room. I stabilised it by cutting and attaching a broom handle. I ended up with two smaller, neater tables from one old ugly one.

INGREDIENTS

- saw
- broom handle
- drill
- screws

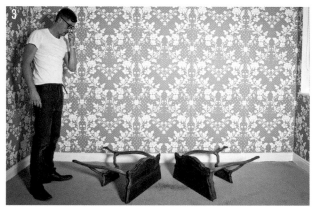

1. & 2. Measure and mark the centre of the tabletop and the under-shelf, and saw them exactly in half.

3. You should now have two symmetrical halves of the table.

4. A plain wooden broom handle will form a stabilising third leg for each table half.

5. Hold the broom handle against your table to measure and mark the required lengths for each new broom-leg to fit between the tabletop and the under-shelf, and between the under-shelf and the floor.

6. Saw the broom handle to four correct lengths.

7. Drill a small pilot hole for the screw at the top of each broom-leg section, as shown.

8. Drill small holes in the table where you want to position the broom-legs. You will need to offset the top and bottom legs so that you can screw each in place – the lower leg should be set slightly further in than the upper leg to allow room for the tables to sit right up against a wall if there is a skirting board.

9. Countersinking the top screw will provide a nicer finish to the table.

10. Attach the bottom leg section first.

11. Attach the upper section of the broom-leg. Repeat for the other table half.

12. The tables can be used on their own placed up against a wall (or as matching bedside tables) and also as trestle supports, as shown.

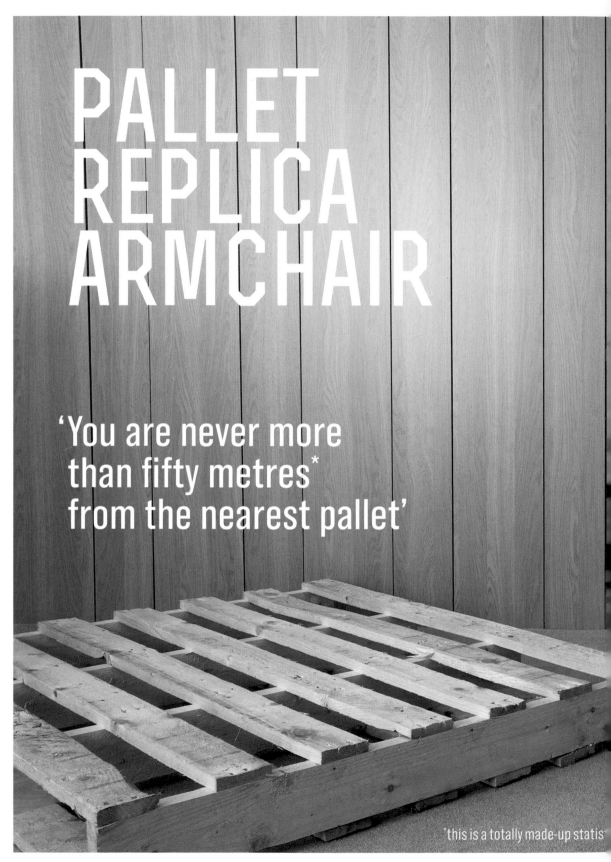

PALLET REPLICA ARMCHAIR

'You are never more than fifty metres* from the nearest pallet'

*this is a totally made-up statis

The Europallet is a design classic. It is considered as a unit or measurement. It has its own international standard number (ISO 6780) but it does also come in different sizes depending where and how it is to be used. Its construction aids transportation by allowing forklift trucks to lift full pallets. Most pallets are made from fast-growing, low-density softwood and because they are considered as packaging, are mostly discarded or recycled. You can often find pallets in skips or collect them for free (or for a small fee) from recycling centres.

I'm aware that lot of furniture has been created using pallet wood, as a quick Internet search will demonstrate. My goal with this project was to design and make a replica of an existing armchair using rough pallet wood, and make it really comfortable. The pallet that you find might not be identical to the one I used, so you might need to adapt the design slightly to suit your particular materials. There are a few critical dimensions and angles crucial to the comfort of the design. To get these angles accurate and ensure a really good and comfortable end result, use the photos on pp. 118–121, placing your wood over the actual-size templates.

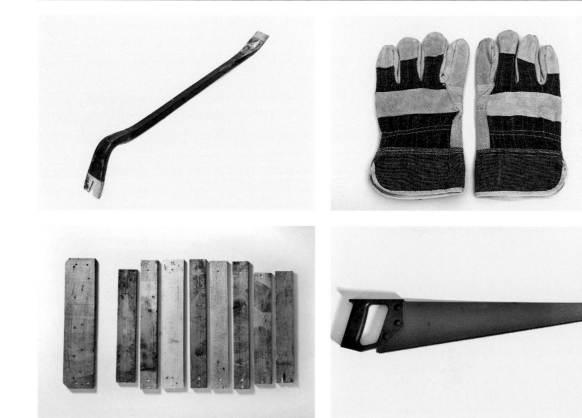

The wood is very sturdy but it was rough and splintery so it could look better sanded or painted. I paid a lot of attention to the design details at the joints to ensure that the design appeared as uncluttered as possible. I also added a leather cowskin at the end to effectively turn it into a leather armchair. Other than that and the cost of the screws, the chair cost absolutely nothing to make.

INGREDIENTS

- crowbar
- gloves (optional)
- pallet
- saw
- drill
- screwdriver
- screws
- animal hide, cushions or a throw

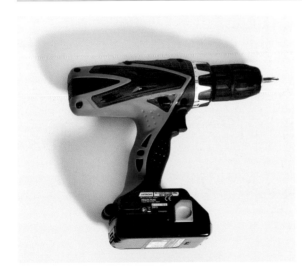

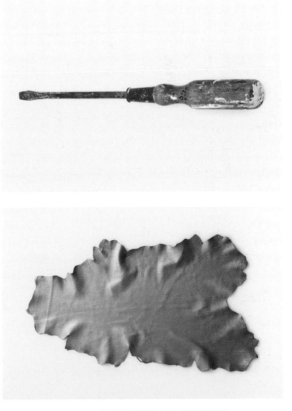

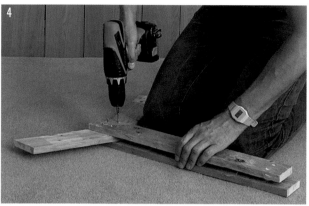

1. Use a crowbar to dismantle the pallet. Wear gloves to avoid splinters.

2. You will soon have a pile of useable timber.

3. I worked out the parts I would need for the replica of my chair and used a saw to cut the wood pieces and the angles accordingly.

4. There are two crucial angles and measurements to calculate – the seat height and angle and the seat-back angle. See the actual-size templates on pp. 118–121.

5. Use a drill and driver to screw the timber components together. Assemble both chair sides.

6. Attach the front cross piece to the chair sides.

7. Attach the cross piece to the chair back – the chair will now stand upright and and make the job easier.

8. Attach cross pieces to make the chair seat.

9. Screw on the smaller wood sections to the chair sides so it is double thickness for strength.

10. Add animal hide, cushions or a throw for extra luxury.

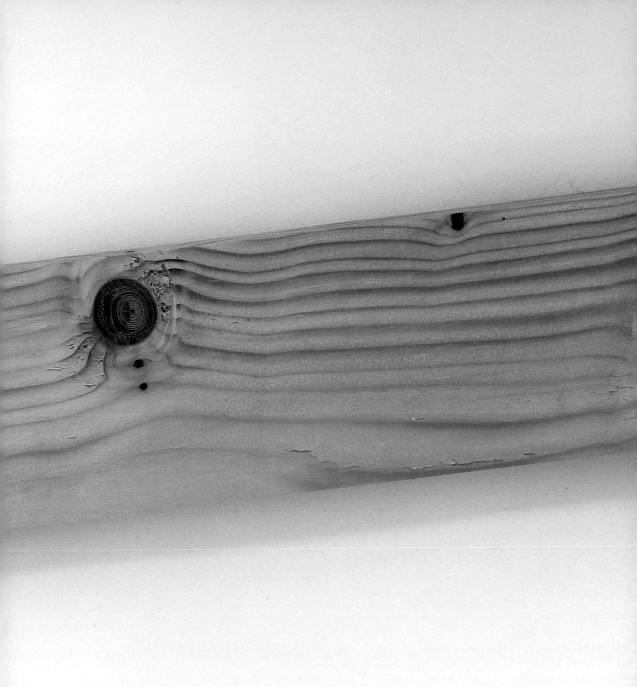

EXTRAORDINARY PROJECTS FROM ORDINARY TASTE

The Hairy Chair
The Wood Car
Hairclips
The Staircase

Taste, along with judgement and decision-making, is often what designers are paid for. But it's a tricky thing to write about. Defining what taste is, and what is good or bad taste, is not an easy task. I was trying to work out where my own sense of taste comes from and I think it's all to do with the type of exposure I have had to objects, colours and patterns in my life and the connections I've made with them. I think it's the same for most people: a particular type of chair, or perhaps the colour of a carpet, might remind you of your childhood and this can trigger good or bad feelings.

My own sense of taste is displayed on every page of this book. Hopefully you can see that already, and you may like or dislike it. It is, of course, entirely subjective. There is bland, safe and conservative taste and more edgy, extreme taste, but ultimately there is no right or wrong. Not being ashamed of what you like is a good rule to live by as long as you let other people do that too. I have quite strong instincts about what I like and what I don't like, but I always try to back up the reasons for my reactions to something: what it reminds me of and the logic behind my desire to change it. I never think it's enough to simply say, 'I like it' or 'I don't like it'.

In some ways it would be good not to worry or be concerned about the way something looks, but unfortunately as a designer I can't help it. Function is always the most important thing for me when it comes to design, but form or aesthetics can make me really love an object. It was my car that really started me thinking about this. My Honda Civic fulfils all my needs: it's efficient, reliable, spacious, practical, versatile, easy to clean. As it was already a bit scratched and dented when I got it, I've never been too precious about it. But that burgundy colour reminded me of something very boring from growing up in the 1980s. I am not sure what, but that is the taste connection that I made. And that is why it was important for me to change how the car looked so I was happier with it.

The projects are all solutions to the problem of my disliking the appearance of something; an answer for things that might be perfect in terms of function, but, well, are bad taste.

THE HAIRY CHAIR

'This chair is really comfortable. This chair is also really ugly'

With stores offering us 'pay nothing until...' deals, we can all now own things we cannot really afford. Very tempting. We used to have to be content with owning something much cheaper, even if it didn't really meet our exact needs or desires. Sofas and armchairs are a really good example of this.

A three-piece suite is one of the most expensive things we will buy for our home, yet replacing it is common when people move house or trends and fashions change.

I was offered this chair by someone who was replacing their suite and I needed a comfy armchair. It's certainly comfortable, and it's well made, with good-quality fabric. But it has flowers on it. To be fair, it is not to my taste. And to be honest, it's hideous and ugly.

At this point I have two options. One is to sulk about the fact that I cannot afford the armchair I *really* want, and start thinking seriously about those furniture deals on TV. The second, is to acknowledge that it's a perfectly good chair and do something to change its appearance (which is really what bothers me).

INGREDIENTS

- chair
- tagging gun
- tags
- laces

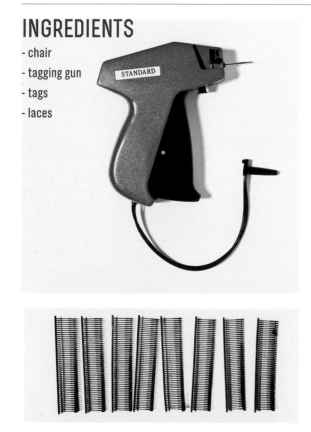

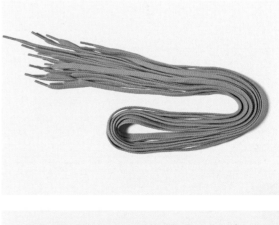

Re-upholstering the chair is not an option: I don't have time to teach myself how to upholster, it would take forever to do it properly and wouldn't really change the appearance of the chair anyway – it would still be a boring chair but with less flowery fabric.

My solution was this re-upholstering made easy technique using a very ordinary, cheap material. I used shoelaces, but you could use jersey tubes, thick wool or some other kind of stringy material. I needed to work out how to attach the shoelaces to the chair: I don't have high patience levels, and so progress needed to be quite fast.

So, I bought a tagging gun, used to price tag garments and the shortest tags available. Both were very cheap and simple to use.

I wanted to group the colours together (rather than blend them): I like asymmetry, and I wanted to offset the symmetry of the chair. The chair took about four or five hours to complete and used about 4000 shoelaces. Yes, it was quite monotonous, but the pay-off was immensely satisfying as the transformation of this large object is gradual but intense. The method is very easy to follow and can be adapted to suit any type of sofa or armchair.

1. Use a tagging gun to spear the needle through the shoelace.

2. & 3. Start near the bottom of the chair and work upwards. The laces should trail, but not too much – about 15cm is ideal. Insert the needle into the upholstery and shoot!

4. Persevere and keep adding the laces approximately 2cm apart.

5. I clumped the blue, orange and brown laces together to form contrasting solid blocks of colour, rather than mixing them all in together.

6. Keep working your way across the upholstery.

7. The result should mean that the ugly fabric is completely covered.

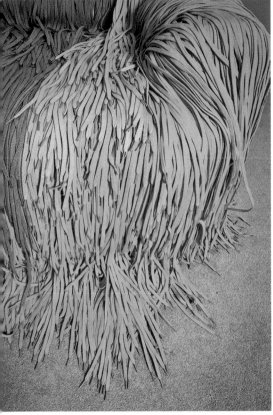

8. You can use strips of jersey, ribbon or rope if you can't get hold of industrial quantities of matching laces.

THE WOOD CAR

'When you have a wooden car, people are really nice to you, they smile and look happy'

My car is fantastic, but when I first got it, I hated it. It's fantastic because it is simply the most reliable car I have ever owned. I can fit almost anything into it, from long pieces of fencing to huge plants. Over the past few years I have also used it as a mobile skip while taking my house apart and transporting rubbish to the tip.

I hated it because it was my least favourite colour...burgundy. (It says 'Red' on the insurance document.)

I needed to buy a car because my motorbike was scary to ride on motorways and I needed to carry stuff to build with. My friend Richard was selling his car and he'd had it from new so I knew he would have looked after it well. I bought it out of necessity, not choice. It already had one or two minor bumps and scratches, which in a way was a good thing because it meant that I wasn't at all precious about it being perfect – I could relax.

Still, I hated how the car looked.

As you have probably worked out by now, I love tape and stickers and I have always been fascinated with sticky-back plastic, so I started to imagine what my car might look like in wood.

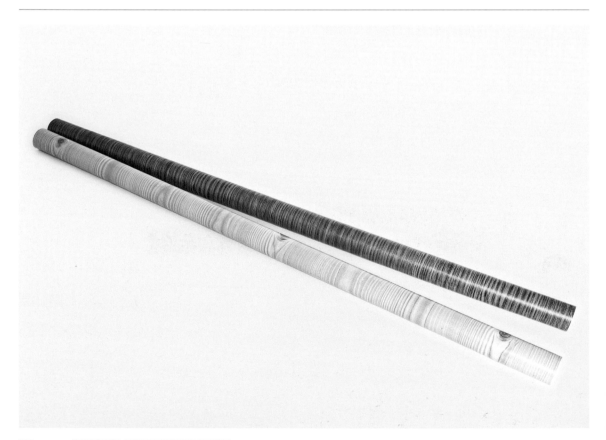

From rolls of Fablon® (sticky-back plastic) I cut out 700 stickers approximately 20cm x 10cm. This is enough to cover the whole car. I used 'knotty pine' for the main sticker as it looks like archetypal wood, but also threw in a few odd sections of 'rustic oak' to vary the pattern.

What I have ended up with is a car which looks like it is a wooden toy car...I love it. I love it even more now, because the Honda Civic is a very popular car for Boy Racers to customise and pimp by lowering the suspension, tinting the glass and adding accessories. So I have created an object that blurs the lines between tastes.

INGREDIENTS

- sticky-back vinyl (e.g. Fablon®)
- craft knife
- car

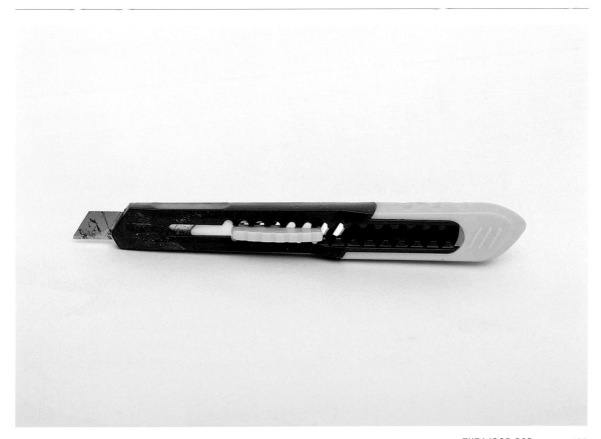

Note. Start at the REAR of the vehicle and work forwards, so that the vinyl is streamlined and won't start to peel on impact with the air when driving. I learnt this through trial and error!

1. Cut the sticky-backed vinyl into 20cm x 10cm (approx.) pieces.

2. Peel off the backing paper.

3. Starting at the rear, apply to the clean surface of the car, smoothing on with the palm of the hand to attach firmly. Make sure there are no bubbles or wrinkles.

4. Continue to add pieces of vinyl. Make sure each piece overlaps the adjacent piece slightly so the whole surface is covered with no gaps.

5. Don't try to work round details on the car or the door handles or lights.

6. Simply use a craft knife to trim and peel away excess vinyl round the details.

7. Continue to add more vinyl sheets at different angles.

8. If your stickers cover a door opening, simply slice through the vinyl at the opening with the craft knife.

9. Open the door and smooth down the vinyl firmly at the door edges.

10. Cover as much of the car, or as little, as you want (I think more is better).

11. & 12. I used a few pieces of darker wood-effect vinyl, here and there, to add contrast.

HAIRCLIPS

USED TO THE POINT WHERE TASTE NO LONGER MATTERS

'Children have a lot
of choice these days,
I only see one option'

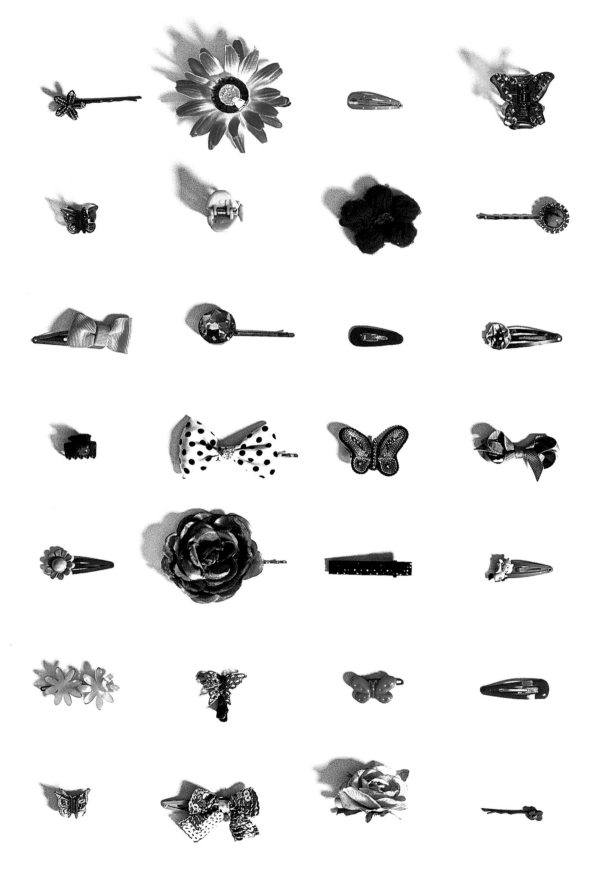

ORDINARY MADE EXTRAORDINARY

Kids seem to have a lot of everything these days. I think if you are eight years old and you have a bike, a scooter, a skateboard, roller blades, roller skates and wheels in your shoes, the chances are that you're never going to be really good, skilled and passionate about any one of them. Too much choice and too many options really can limit progress as we flit from one thing to the next without experiencing any form of perseverance.

Decision-making can lead to a similar inertia, too many choices and dithering about which choice might be best, in the worst case not choosing at all. This project addresses all this. What happens when we take something ordinary, like a hairclip, but use it in a way that we wouldn't normally think of? I used 100 hairclips to cover the whole head, creating a hairclip 'helmet'.

INGREDIENTS

- hairclips

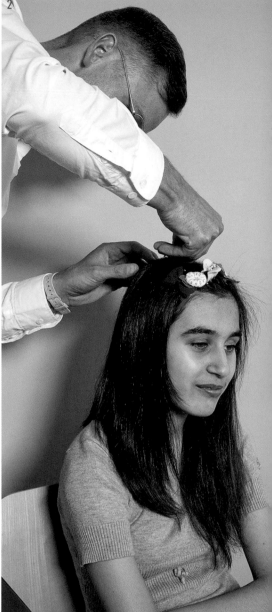

1. Make sure that your model is comfortably seated.
2. Start to pin the hairclips in a random fashion.
3. Start at the front and work backwards.
4. Pick up and add in lengths of hair as you work round the head.

5. The aim is to clip all the hair up and to cover the head with clips. Again, don't worry about which clip goes where.
6. Continue to work round the head until all the clips are used and, for maximum effect, make sure no sign of hair is visible.

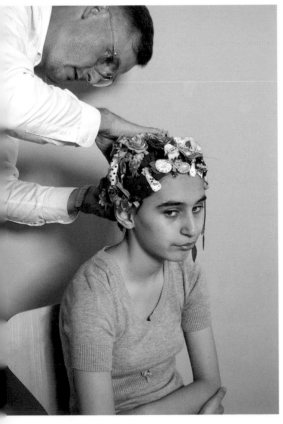

THE STAIRCASE

'I can't afford a carpet – and don't really like carpets anyway'

I was excited at the thought of designing and constructing a staircase for my new roof extension. The staircase had to fit tightly into a small space, not take up too much room and be well detailed to fit in with the existing structure. It was a challenge but I was happy with the look and function of the end result.

I didn't have enough money to carpet the staircase and wasn't sure that I wanted carpet in any case, although it would have had really good soundproofing qualities. I was also keen to experiment further with adhesive tape.

I began collecting adhesive tapes about five years ago, and in every country I visit I seek out hardware stores and art supplies shops to see what kind of tape that country sells. I've ended up with quite a considerable collection and was very aware that I wanted to put my collection to good use, not just keep it in a box. I thought that the staircase would be a good place to experiment. I think you can be a little more experimental with small transitional spaces like hallways and stairs.

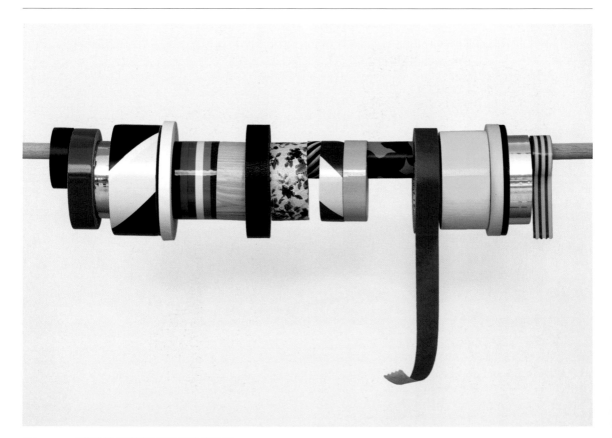

I like the artist Jim Lambie's tape installations, but I wanted to use tape in a slightly less formal way and come up with an idea that everyone could try. So I imagined what it would be like if tape behaved like a liquid and what a spill of magic, multi-coloured paint would look like if it ran down a flight of stairs. That's what prompted my first video and I animated the tape to make it look like spilled paint. That's the inspiration for this idea.

It's quite easy to do, and if you are careful the magic tape carpet can last a reasonably long time, but it is a temporary solution. In the context of my home it leads the eye into a special small room which just has a sofa and a view of the sky, perfect for drinking a cup of tea and for quiet contemplation.

INGREDIENTS
- tape
- credit card
- craft knife
- set square
- circle cutter

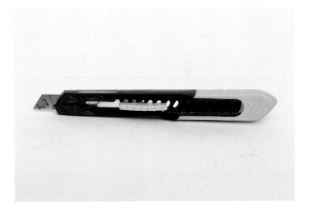

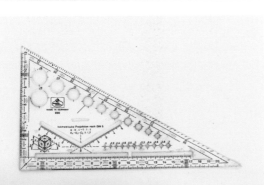

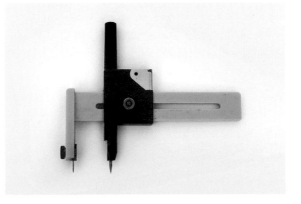

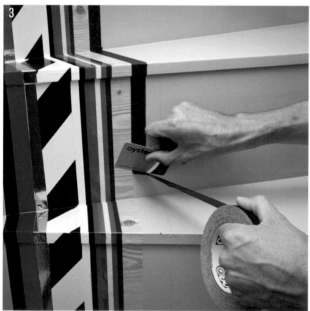

1. Start with clean, dust-free stairs. You don't have to paint them! Begin at the top of the stairs, at any point, and with any tape.

2. Keep some tension in the tape to make sure there are no wrinkles or bumps. Don't try to co-ordinate your colour choices. A random mix of widths, lengths and colours works best. Trust me.

3. Work your way down, applying the tape in straight lines. Use a credit card to get rid of bubbles and smooth the tape down, right into the angles under each step.

4. You can work step by step, or in sections – you don't have to do the whole run in one continuous strip.

5. A turn in the stairs will make it harder to keep the tape straight. If you're finding it hard to get the angle right, simply cut the tape, adjust, and continue. Use a set square to keep things tight.

6. Play with different lengths – here I wanted to make it look like magical paint had spilled down the stairs.

7. Ensure each new run of tape is tightly aligned to the adjoining tape.

8. You can use a circle cutter to give a neat finish to the ends.

9. Make sure the tape is stuck down well to help protect against wear and tear – avoid stiletto heels! Tape stairs should stand the test of time, but they work best on low-traffic areas.

EXTRAORDINARY PROJECTS FROM ORDINARY OBJECTS

Part of the role of a designer is to analyse objects – in order to make existing ones better, or to devise completely new ones which hopefully make life better. I am constantly questioning the objects I encounter; I examine, I test, I dismantle, I shake, I squeeze. This is analysis. I am also fascinated by how resourceful people can be, using objects for purposes for which they were never intended. I call this 'reappropriation'.

Analysis and careful examination allows me to take something apart, and then thinking as a designer allows me put it back together again differently to perform a new function. This is about being open-minded and being driven by the possibilities and potential that the world can offer us if we don't adhere to convention. Not everything works first time, ambitious failure is often the best way to make stuff work better the second time.

Most of the projects in the book are very easy to follow, and I have shown the design process needed to transform the objects into new ones. But it is my hope that you too are starting to see objects differently and see other possible potential uses and reinventions.

The key question to ask of every object is: 'What happens if?' This is a creative question, but you can only ask 'What if?', if you are open to possibly ridiculous answers.

THE STILTS

'Sometimes you have to think stupid to make clever'

ORDINARY MADE EXTRAORDINARY

We use stools and chairs to climb on to reach shelves and change light bulbs. The Frosta stool from Ikea is a copy of Alvar Aalto's three-legged *Stool 60* from 1932. Presumably to avoid copyright issues they added another leg. This is fortunate as it inspired me to think about using the stool and reconfiguring it in a new way.

I took the legs off the stool and joined them in pairs to make a pair of child's stilts – they are about 40cm high and are attached to the child using gaffer tape.

INGREDIENTS
- IKEA stool
- electric screwdriver
- small person
- tape

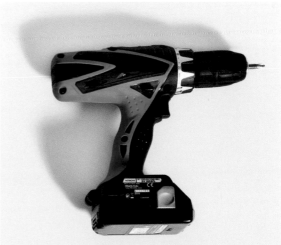

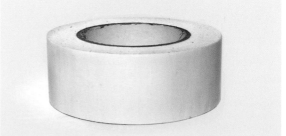

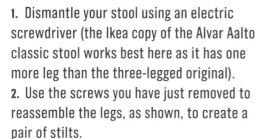

1. Dismantle your stool using an electric screwdriver (the Ikea copy of the Alvar Aalto classic stool works best here as it has one more leg than the three-legged original).
2. Use the screws you have just removed to reassemble the legs, as shown, to create a pair of stilts.

3. Make sure that each pair of legs is securely screwed together, then position the small person's feet and legs on the stilts, as shown.
4. & 5. Use strong gaffer tape to fit the stilts securely to the small person.

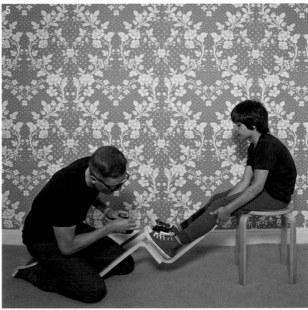

6. Wind the gaffer tape round each leg and stilt several times. Test, and make sure there is absolutely no give at all between the small person's leg and stilt.

7. Help the small person to stand upright on their stilts.

N.B. Adult supervision is recommended at all times while the small person is sporting these stilts.

CONCRETE PLANTER

'Look at things differently – turn them upside down to see if they make more sense!'

I have become quite good at getting orchids to re-bloom. I don't pay them that much attention: I think it's more to do with where they are in my studio. South-facing but with filtered light through a blind, they seem to thrive. I read somewhere that Phalenopsis orchids photosynthesise in their recovery phase through their roots as well as through their leaves and that's why they come in transparent pots. Once flowering they can be placed in an opaque pot.

I was looking at food containers such as plastic milk cartons and treat tubs and thinking that the polypropylene plastic they are made from is perfect for casting moulds, as nothing sticks to it. This is for hygiene reasons in food packaging but also good for other purposes.

An empty tub of post-workout powder turned upside down has an interesting shape and I decided to see what it would look like if I cast it in ordinary concrete to make a pot. I used a smaller treat tub to make the cavity for the plant to sit in. The concrete was ordinary ready to mix cement which is very cheap and available from any hardware or DIY shop.

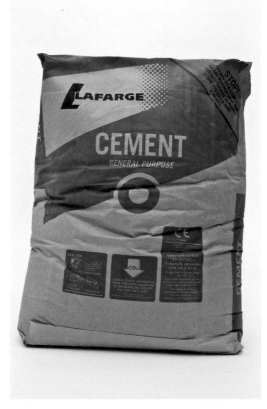

I also invested in a mixing whisk, because, to be honest, the hardest part was mixing the concrete to the correct consistency. Mixing whisks are fairly inexpensive and I found it really helped.

INGREDIENTS

- cement mix
- a bucket or two
- water for mixing
- mixing whisk
- 2 empty food tubs
- scissors
- brick or bottle of water

1. Put some dry concrete into a clean bucket (the quantity depends on how tall you want your pot to be). I recommend 5kg – about $\frac{1}{5}$ or $\frac{1}{4}$ of a bag.

2. Add water, following the packet instructions. I usually add less water than I think, then mix and add more as I go.

3. Mix until the concrete is smooth. I use a mixing whisk (available from any hardware store), but you can use a stick – it just takes longer to get the lumps out.

4. & 5. Turn a protein powder (or similar) tub with a lid upside down and cut off the bottom with strong scissors.

6. Carefully pour the concrete into the inverted tub. Make sure the lid is on properly!

7. 8. & 9. Take a second smaller tub (make sure it is large enough to hold your flowerpot) and press it down into the mixture, displacing some of the concrete. Make sure that the small tub is nicely centered then weight it down using a heavy object. Leave for 24 hours.

10. & 11. Once fully set, squeeze the smaller tub to release and remove.

12. & 13. Remove the outer tub, cutting down either side with scissors or a Stanley knife.

14. Unscrew and remove the tub lid. Ease the plastic away.

15. The bottom is trickier to remove as the plastic is thicker. Take your time and be careful if you're using a knife.

THE
GO
SIGN

'Road signs remind me of pop art from the 1960s: simple, bold and graphic'

I have never really thought too hard about what to put up on the walls at home. Before I reach that stage, I seem to move on to another part of the house that needs modifying or repairing. Both my parents are painters and so I was used to having original artworks and prints around when I was growing up. That said, I've never really wanted to hang oil paintings on my walls. I much prefer interesting objects.

Certain very ordinary objects can be so aesthetically pleasing that I forget their everyday function and practical use. This is what happened with the Stop/Go sign. I found it in a car park at Greenford tube station, lying scratched and dented from use and misuse (I think quite a few cars must have also driven over it). Road signs always remind me of pop art from the 1960s: simple, bold, colourful and graphic. Their surface is really beautiful: they are printed with a special reflective paint to show up in car headlights, but the scratched detail on my sign made it even better.

So I picked it up and took it to a picture framer. I chose to have the 'Go' side facing out as I thought that was more me than 'Stop'! In its frame, it looked even better than I hoped. When you frame anything it automatically turns into something special. Pretty much any object can look good when framed and hung on a wall – it is de-contextualised and becomes art. Something you'd like to look at and for other people to look at differently.

This is nothing new. Think of Marcel Duchamp exhibiting his urinal in 1917. The art is in the choice of object, and that is accessible to everyone. I hope this project will inspire you to find something that you find interesting, an object or thing that is beautiful possibly only through your eyes, and to frame or hang it to make a statement, and give it value.

INGREDIENTS
- hammer
- nail
- interesting thing

MOTH JACKET

'A good jacket to wear to a funeral'

ORDINARY MADE EXTRAORDINARY

I hate black, on the whole. I feel really, well, dead when I am wearing black. It's such a cliché designer colour. I appreciate all the arguments for having lots of black clothes, texture, fabric, knit, silhouette and so on, but I am not a fan. I do realise, however, that sometimes there are occasions when something formal (often black) is necessary.

I bought a very nicely fitting dinner jacket on the sale rail one January for £10. I had already made the butterfly shoes, a project which is essentially about repair. With the jacket I just wanted to change its appearance because although it fitted

beautifully, it was just dull. And because I hadn't paid much money for it, I was not at all precious about what happened to it.

I sprayed the left-over butterfly patches black and grey, essentially turning them into slightly more sinister moths, and then sewed on some black safety pins which I bought on eBay, which added a nice detail and also meant that the embellishment could be temporary, and allow for removal or adjustments. The black spray paint also makes the butterflies somewhat stiffer. The jacket became quite a macabre piece, quite haute couture and far removed from its high

INGREDIENTS

- jacket
- safety pins
- butterfly patches
- needle
- thread
- paper
- black and grey spray paints

street origin. For me, when I wear it, it sits on the borderline of costume and occasion. It is sombre and understated enough to wear to a funeral and at the same time unusual enough to wear to a special occasion.

1. Start by carefully attaching the safety pins to the back of the each patch. Ideally, sew each pin on by hand, but a glue gun will also work as long as you do it carefully.

2. Place the butterfly patches on some sheets of newspaper and spray well on the front and back with black or dark grey spray paint.

3. You might need a few coats to cover them completely.

4. You now have moths. Leave to dry thoroughly.

5. Pin the moths on to the shoulders of your jacket.

6. The safety pins allow you to reposition the moths until you get them just where you want them.

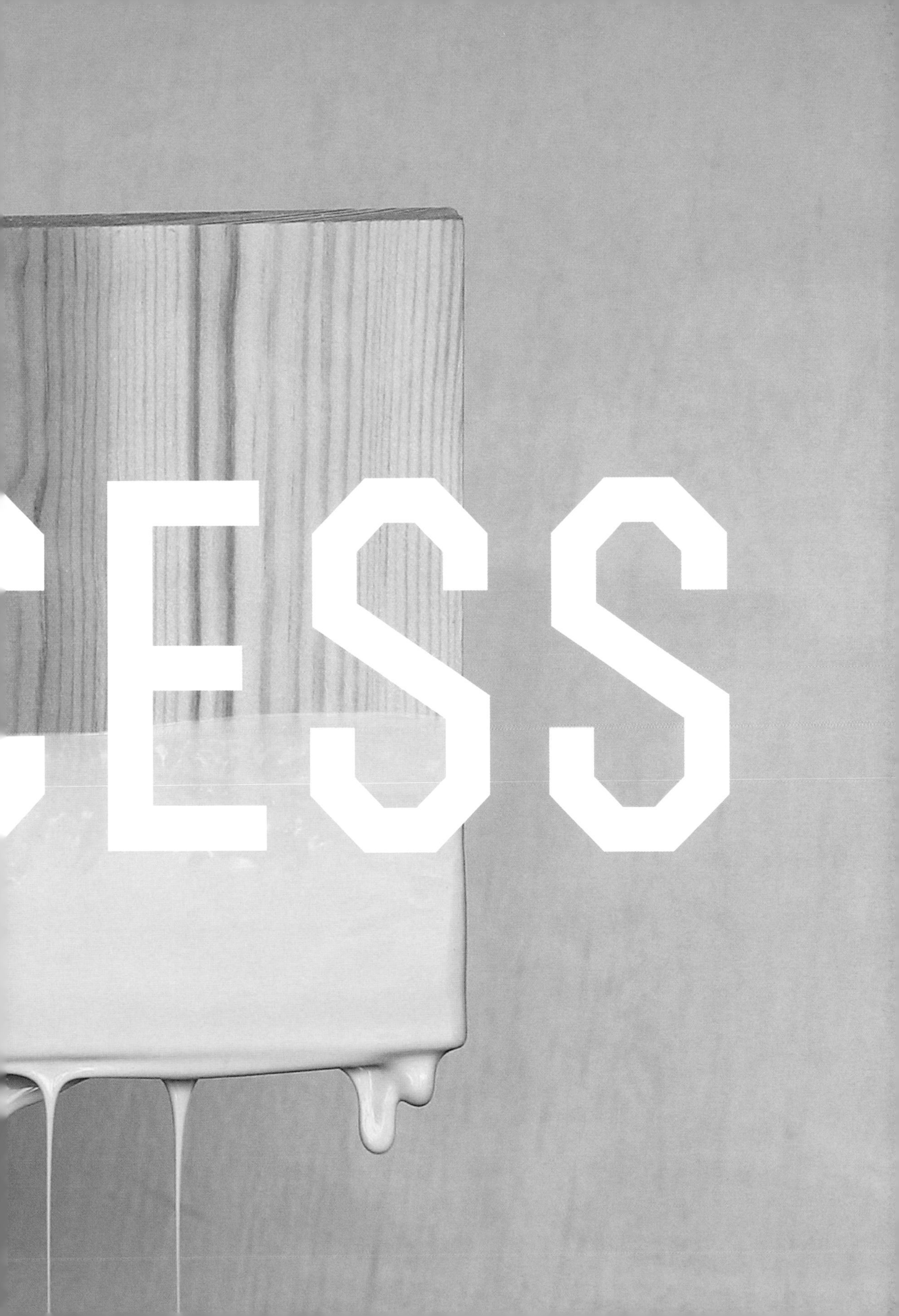
CESS

EXTRAORDINARY PROJECTS FROM ORDINARY PROCESSES

Concrete Cup Stool
T-Shirt Printing
The Perfect Circle
Photocopier Wallpaper

Possibly the first creative process we learn as children is one of destruction. Our first instinct as we explore and test the material world, is to exert our power over an object or material to tear it, break it, smash it, divide it, shred it, scrunch it and rip it apart. Later, we progress to more controlled processes like cutting with scissors or breaking with a hammer. We make a tool with a process and then that tool often becomes the next stage in the process. It is an innate human practice to take a big thing and make it smaller and more refined by chipping, whittling, crushing, grinding, shredding, or engraving. These are all reductive processes that humans use to modify materials to make them do what they need. Some processes like knitting or weaving use tools to perform the opposite function: combining small pieces of a material into a larger one. Other processes like casting provide us with the opportunity to make facsimiles.

Over millennia we have invented ever more sophisticated ways to manipulate materials and the things around us. Today rapid prototype machines, laser cutters and computers process and transform materials for us. We all use processes at home and at work every day, from using the photocopier to make multiple documents in the workplace, to the lawnmower cutting the grass and the lemon-squeezer squeezing lemons in the kitchen.

Look around you right now and see how many tools and machines you can see, from nail clippers, to a pencil sharpener, to your toaster. Now, let's start to think about what else we might be able to accomplish with them. Can I heat, melt and bend plastic over a toaster, if I were to use it like a strip heater? Other than my smoothie, what else could I mix using the hand blender? And what can I attach to the end of my power drill other than a drill bit?

We take most of these things and their functions for granted, so this chapter is about looking at some ordinary processes afresh – such as cutting and photocopying – and putting them to use them in an extraordinary and creative way.

These processes are often very simple ones that we have all done many times before. The hard part is thinking a little differently about how to apply these processes in both new and interesting ways.

CONCRETE CUP STOOL

'Coffee cups, concrete and sitting down on your coffee break'

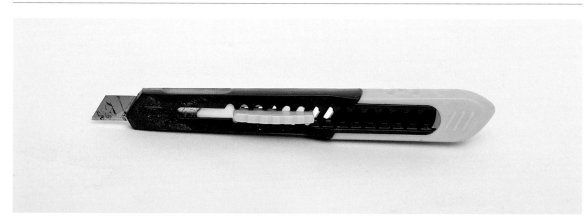

I wanted to experiment with concrete casting, but I wanted a mould that was easy to use and readily available and a casting process which was equally simple. Paper cups are coated with a waxy layer which makes them waterproof. This, and their tapered shape, also makes them ideal casting moulds. The form reminded me of some of the sculptor Brancusi's work, and I decided to experiment by trying to tessellate the forms to make a stool. I started off using small cups as moulds and the stool was too small. The ideal seating height is a minimum 40cm, so on my next attempt I used fewer, larger cups to achieve the result. This idea is pretty fail-safe.

To be honest, the hardest part was mixing the concrete to the correct consistency; the mixing whisk really helped. I love this stool – and because it's made of concrete it's completely weatherproof, making it perfect for balconies or the garden.

INGREDIENTS

- craft knife
- cups
- tape
- cement mix
- bucket
- mixing whisk

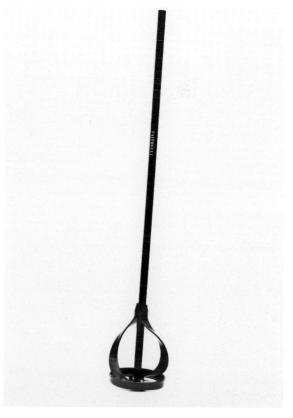

1. Use a craft knife to carefully cut out the bases from six paper cups. Keep three cups intact.

2. & 3. Use thick gaffer tape to join two cups together at the base, as shown.

4. Tape a third paper cup (with its base intact) to the first two, as shown.

5. Mix the concrete in a bucket, following the packet instructions (you need the equivalent of six large lattes).

6. Carefully pour the concrete mix into the three moulds.

7. Leave to dry and set for twenty-four hours. Cut away the paper moulds.

8. You should have three solid concrete 'legs'.

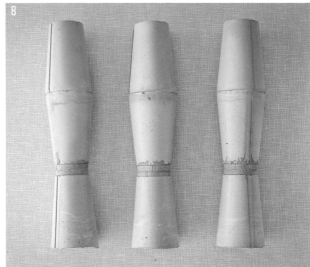

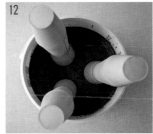

9. To make the stool top, add more concrete mix to a clean empty paint tub or similar.

10. Mix thoroughly – the ideal depth of the mixed concrete in the tub should be about 5cm.

11. Place one leg at a time into the concrete mix.

12. Make sure the legs are evenly spaced.

13. Leave to set overnight.

14. Carefully turn the container upside down and gently release the stool from the mould.

T-SHIRT PRINTING

'What do you see?
Some people
might see a skull,
others a dove.
Some people might
just see blobs of ink'

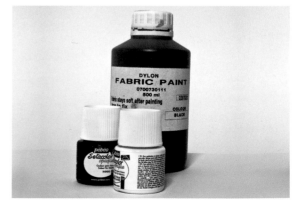

The aesthetics of Rorschach prints are far more compelling than the psychological implications of the ink blot tests that were used in the early 20th century. This printing method works really well, is very easy and gives you a unique garment. Don't be too worried about where you drop the fabric paints, the fun of this project is that the end result is unpredictable and uncontrollable. You can use whatever colours you like, you can use large or small blobs and spread the paint all over the garment, or just in one area.

INGREDIENTS

- paper
- t-shirt
- pencil
- fabric paint
- chopping board
- Coke bottle (optional)
- iron

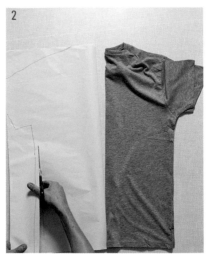

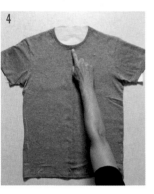

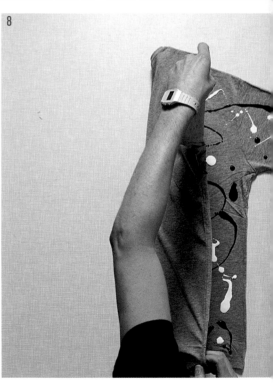

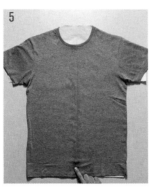

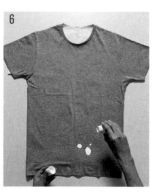

1. Place several large sheets of paper or newspaper on a flat surface. Lay the plain t-shirt flat on the paper and roughly trace around it with a pencil.

2. Fold the layers of paper in half vertically and cut 1cm INSIDE the line you have just drawn.

3. Unfold, and slide the layers of paper inside the t-shirt to prevent the fabric paint from seeping through to the back of the fabric.

4. & 5. Make sure that the centre crease in the paper sits in the centre of the neck opening and the bottom hem of the t-shirt. (For accuracy, you can fold the t-shirt in half lengthwise and iron the crease.)

6. 7. & 8. Add some blobs of fabric paint to one side of the t-shirt and fold it in half lengthwise.

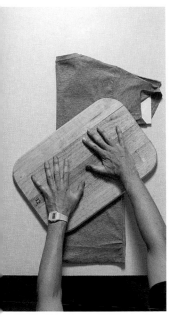

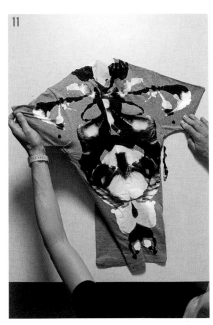

9. Press firmly down on the folded over t-shirt with a flat, heavy object (I used a chopping board) so that the paint is transferred evenly on both sides of the fabric.

10. You can also use a full drinks bottle and use it like a rolling pin, pressing down firmly and evenly.

11. Carefully peel the t-shirt apart and leave it to dry. Do not remove the paper inside.

12. When the fabric paint is DRY place a clean sheet of paper over the design.

13. Iron the shirt through the paper on a high setting, making sure you cover the entire surface to fix the fabric paint.

14. Remove the paper from the top and inside of the shirt.

THE PERFECT CIRCLE

'As a kid, drawing the perfect circle was always a perfect challenge'

ORDINARY MADE EXTRAORDINARY

ORDINARY MADE EXTRAORDINARY

I can remember being fascinated by drawing circles at school. They were always so difficult to get right...well, perfect. This project allows everyone to draw a perfect circle. Use one large piece of paper, or join smaller pieces together, stand below the middle of the page and use your whole arm to draw the circle. You can use whatever pens, pencils or crayons you like.

INGREDIENTS

- paper
- felt-tip pens

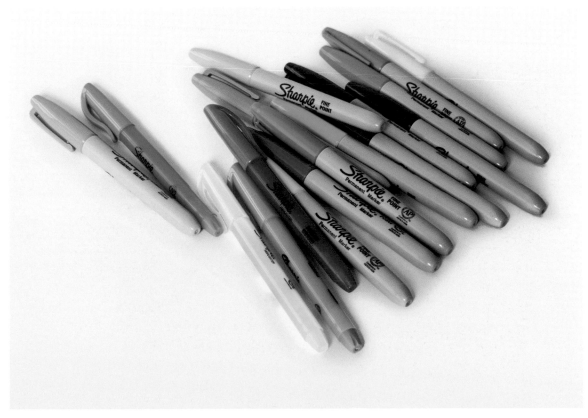

1. Attach a large, clean piece of paper to a wall with tape.

2. With a felt-tip pen in your hand, stand next to the paper with your shoulder in the centre of the page.

3. With your arm at full stretch, make sure that the tip of your pen is still on the page (and you're not about to draw on the wallpaper).

4. Keep your arm fully extended and straight, and begin to slowly draw the biggest circle you can.

5. Continue forming circles with your arm at full stretch, changing pen to a different colour every ten revolutions or so.

6. The order or choice of colours doesn't really matter, but my tip is to start with the lighter colours and not to use a black felt tip.

7. After you have used each colour in your
pack of twenty-four felt tips (or thereabouts)
you should have a perfect circle.

PHOTOCOPIER WALLPAPER

'Prepare it in your lunch break – paste it at the weekend!'

When I was a teenager, I had a Saturday job in South London and the office had a photocopier which I used to love playing with when the managers weren't looking. It made photocopies with a really good dense black coating of toner ink. I can remember being very interested in how the process worked and loved experimenting with printing on different papers and reducing and enlarging stuff.

I'd wanted to use a billboard poster to wallpaper an interior for some time, but then I came up with this idea which fulfils both needs for scale and ease. The photocopied wallpaper image is big enough to cover a whole wall with two doors – the inspiration for using the wallpaper as *trompe l'oeil* came from a visit to Buckingham Palace – when I needed the bathroom I had to ask a footman to point the way and a door magically appeared from what I first thought was a wall. I wanted to use a standard photocopier with normal settings so I looked in a comic book for a strong black and white image which would photocopy well and bought some yellow A3 paper from an office supplies store. The mathematics was the most complicated part of this project (I am quite bad at maths), but once I'd worked out the scale it was surprisingly easy.

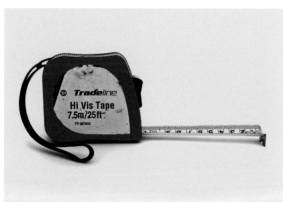

Calculate how many A3 or A4 sheets will fill your wall, and whether they are to be portrait or landscape. Work out how many times larger the wall area is than your original image. Make as few enlargement steps as possible; most copiers enlarge 400%. A3 is 400% larger than A7, so enlarge your original to the point where it is made up of lots of A7 size pieces.

I used regular wallpaper paste to hang the sheets to the wall – it was quick work and I wasn't too concerned about it being perfectly smooth and accurate. The size and scale of the image has a lot of impact on the room.

INGREDIENTS

- tape measure
- photocopier
- paper
- roller
- wallpaper paste
- scissors
- craft knife
- pen

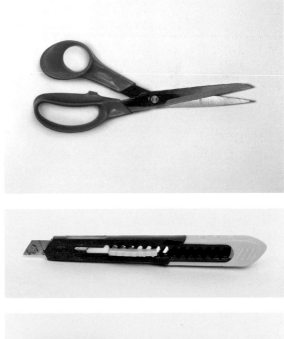

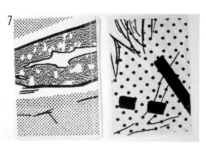

1. Measure and note the width of your wall in EITHER millimetres or centimetres (not a combination).

2. Measure and note the wall height.

3. Make some calculations!

4. Select an image from a favourite comic or book.

5. Photocopy the image following your calculations.

6. I used an A3 coloured office copy-paper.

7. Keep the printed sheets in the correct sequence as you copy. This will make things easier later on.

8. Use a roller and wallpaper paste to liberally coat the back of the copy paper.

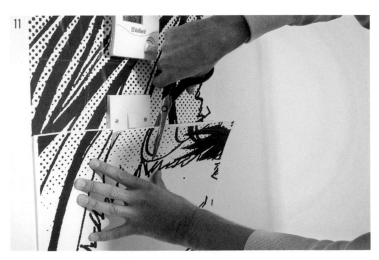

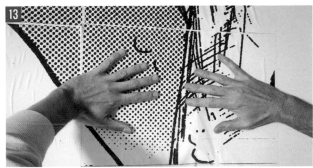

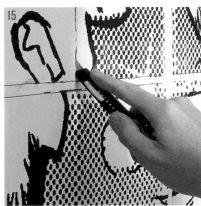

9. Paste the first section of your image to the wall, making sure it is perfectly straight (this is crucial as the correct positioning of this first section will affect the alignment of the rest of the sequence). Wear work overalls or your pyjamas.

10. Paste each of the rest of the copies to the wall in sequence.

11. Cut neatly around light switches and wall sockets.

12. Smooth out any air bubbles as you go.

13. & 14. Work methodically from top to bottom.

15. Use a craft knife to carefully slice around any doors in the wall.

16. Use a thick black marker pen to fill in any gaps and details.

ACKNOWLEDGEMENTS

DISCARD

All these people have been supportive in different
ways, helping me to put this book together:

Mark Vessey

Doug Kerr

Anoushka Monzon Ladas

Nicolai Monzon Ladas

Nadia Demetriou Ladas

Roshan Higgins

Lubna Chowdhary

Alan Spink

Neil Grosvenor

Kevin O'Neill

Henri Swift

Sam Chapman

Angel Monzon

Ben Harries

Sarah Dyer's Legs

Claude Mauk

Rasputin Thorpedo

Russell John

Jasper Morrison

Jodi Mullen

Michelle Edwards

Zeljko Blace

David Forrest

Ian Higgins

Chris Wellbelove

Paul Burt

Rosemary Davidson

Jan Bowmer

Natalie Wall

Rowena Skelton-Wallace

Ruth Warburton

Kate Bland

Simon Rhodes

Fran Barrie

Will Smith

Helena Roux Dessarps

Olivia Roux Dessarps

Alan Collins

Emily Campbell

Kevin Hemmings

Graham Roberts

Ralph Lillford

Margaret Lillford

Thanks to my mum for casting her critical eye
over everything and making me understand how
to work hard. Thanks to my dad for showing me
how to work fast and helping me not to care
about what anyone else thinks of your work.